# SPIRIT BEASTS AWAKENING

BOOK 1

THE SPIRIT BEAST SAGA

A.P BESWICK

Editing - Quill & Bone Editing

Cover Design - Donn Marlou Ramirez

ISBN - 978-1-916671-11-9

*To the dreamers and believers, remember, you are the masters of your fate; let this tale illuminate the boundless power within you.*

*For the spirited folk of Oswaldtwistle: more real than our ever-present rain and just as enchanting as our resident spirit beasts. Here's to proving we're not a fantasy, but the real magic of the North West!*

# SPIRIT BEASTS

## AWAKENING

## WHAT IS A SPIRIT BEAST

A Spirit Beast is an anchor to someone's soul, it is the other side of a coin. Without one you are simply not complete. To have a Spirit Beast is a gift, their role to guide you through life. It is felt that Spirit Beasts compliment one's strongest personality traits and takes a form to complement this. For some when coming of age and unlocking the power to their Spirit Beasts, they will find that their connection will grant them new abilities.

Not all use this power for good though.

‘

# PROLOGUE

Arnold gasped as the freezing cold air engulfed his lungs, instantly stealing his breath. The sharp, stinging sensation forced him to take rapid, short breaths just to take in enough air.

"In through the nose and out through the mouth," he told himself, recalling the advice he had received on a camping trip with the cub scouts years ago about surviving in the cold, not realising back then that he would actually find it helpful one day.

Once he adapted to the cold, he was able to take in the mesmerising view. The fields below him were illuminated brightly by the haunting crescent moon above, making the adjoining fields look like a complex patchwork quilt. The moonlight created a soft shimmer that made the grass look as though it were water, and the trees seemed to dance in synchronised motion, their branches swaying gracefully to the melody of rushing wind and rustling leaves as if being guided by a composer. Nature's very own orchestra.

Arnold's momentum steadied, and he slowed to an almost complete stop but then suddenly felt as though he was going to fall. An overwhelming sense of panic engulfed him as he felt the fierce force of the wind pushing against him. Nature's choreographer had changed the pace and Arnold needed to respond accordingly. He knew he needed to let the wind pass before he could move on but the icy chill that engulfed him felt as though it were touching every inch of his bones; it was a coldness he had never experienced before. He needed to persevere and ride the incoming gust of pressure generated by the ferocious wind, so he stretched his wings out as far as he could and tilted them at an angle to catch the uplift from the wind. He was very aware of how easy it would be to lose balance and plummet like a rock to the hard, unforgiving ground below. This was an art form; the wind was a natural force and could not be tamed by anybody. He rode the breath of the wind rather than fighting against it, using it to his advantage. The force of the wind made his feathers vibrate against him violently, making it harder for him to focus. He just about managed to keep his wings in position and maintain a gliding stance.

Arnold maintained this focus until the relentless wind subsided, then he changed his position again, gliding downwards at a steady pace to reach the patchwork fields below. Landing on a large branch of an old oak tree, he shook himself to bring all his feathers back into shape. He couldn't help but feel that he must have lost a few of his feathers from his latest experience of night flying. He was still getting accustomed to this. He did not even know what he was, but he had a strong feeling that it was only a matter of time before he found out.

# CHAPTER 1

"What on earth are you on about, Arnold?" Arnold's dad, Bernard, was sat across from Arnold at the beechwood table, his wrinkled forehead giving him a rather puzzled look whilst he bit into his marmalade toast. "Is this another one of your dreams?" Bernard pushed his slightly greying quiffed hair back as he spoke. The radio was playing down the hallway from the kitchen where Arnold's mum, Eve, was making their lunch. She was singing along to *At Last* by Etta James; it was one of her favourites. The smell of slightly burnt toast filled the air, Eve having left the toast slightly too long due to being distracted by the music.

"Yes, it was another dream," Arnold replied through a mouthful of his breakfast cereal, making a mess. His dark, unkempt hair needed some attention before he headed off to school. Arnold's lightly freckled face focused intently on his dad as he wanted to describe every detail he could, his dark brown eyes unmoving. He sat perched at the end of his seat, rapidly tapping his foot on the floor which began to make the table rock. Bernard wasn't giving Arnold his full attention, however, as his eyes drifted over his newspaper.

"Honestly, Dad, it felt so real, like I was actually flying

through the sky!" Noticing his dad's disinterest, Arnold felt a wave of disappointment. "Are you listening to me?" he snapped, feeling a rush of temper come across him.

"Sounds good, son," Bernard murmured, seeming somewhat distracted. He lowered his newspaper and gazed over the top, his glasses sliding to the bottom of his nose. He sighed loudly as he turned the page, the bold letters reading, *The Oswaldtwistle Advertiser*. Underneath was the heading, "Another Doyen Attack – Spirit Wardens Will Not Change Stance." Bernard stared at the paper with his eyebrows lowered, a serious expression on his face.

Eve came in from the kitchen, her mousy brown hair tied up into a bun. She was already dressed for her retail job in her light-blue, polka dot dress uniform. Her thin frame underneath made it very clear who Arnold took after.

She began cleaning up the breakfast table. "Bernard," she prompted with the gentle but stern tone she had perfected, "Arnold is trying to talk to you about his dream." She shook her head, which brought a smug smile to Arnold's face. "If it's about his dreams, you need to listen to what he is saying."

Apparently realising the error of his ways, Bernard made a fake coughing noise and folded up his newspaper, lowering it to the table and placing it next to his half-eaten marmalade on toast. "Sorry, Arnold, what were you saying? It's just that there has been another Doyen attack and it looks as though a group of menial fanatics has taken responsibility for it."

Menial was the term used for somebody who couldn't harness any power from a spirit beast. Being a menial meant you were unable to demonstrate any special talents or traits as a result of being disconnected from the spirit world – something that the Spirit Wardens looked down on. Arnold wasn't a fan of the phrase, but at the same time, his biggest fear was that he was one.

The news momentarily made Arnold forget about his

dream. "Do you definitely think it was a menial?" he asked. It was well-known that menials often sought out artefacts imbued with spirit energy, hoping they'd be granted special talents which, to them, made them equal to Spirit Wardens.

"More than likely is. I mean, who else would want to pinch an artefact?" Bernard responded.

"I would."

"Pardon?"

"If I was a menial, I would want to steal an artefact. It must be horrible not to have a spirit beast. Doesn't even bear thinking about. I wouldn't hurt anyone though," he added hastily, noticing his dad's shocked expression.

"That's a sure way to get on the wrong side of the Spirit Wardens, Arnold. I thought you wanted to be a Doyen?"

Arnold was being deadly serious, though. He had always dreamed of working for the Spirit Wardens. Unfortunately, to be a part of the Spirit Wardens, you needed to demonstrate both spirit beast and talents, and you had to be eighteen. One could not simply apply to join the Spirit Wardens; you had to be invited, and invitations were rare, only given to qualified candidates who demonstrated acts of bravery.

Arnold's powers, however, hadn't manifested yet, and his greatest fear was that they never would. But for as long as he could remember, Arnold had wanted to join the Spirit Wardens and become a Doyen, helping to protect his local community of Oswaldtwistle just as his dad had been doing since he was twenty years old. Bernard had spent his adult life protecting the local community from those that wished to use their talents to harm others.

Arnold had always lived in Oswaldtwistle, an old industrial town in the North of England. Back in the day it was a hub for coal mining as well as playing a key part in the industrial era in the early 1900s. The last of the coal mines had been flooded and sealed up over twenty years ago but many of the original mine entrances could still be seen. Oswaldtwistle was now like most other towns, with schools, local shops, butchers and – in Arnold's opinion – one too many bakeries. The town's claim to fame was that it was home to the world's largest pear drop which was on display at the old sweetshop inside the local factory mill outlet. Every day, wave upon wave of day coaches filled with people wanting to visit the sweet shop and all the other shops inside the old mill would descend on the town. The rest of the factories within Oswaldtwistle lay dormant, these industrial graveyards a constant reminder of the dominant trade that once ran through the very veins of the town.

"I keep having dreams that I am flying, Dad. That's got to be a sign that my spirit beast is going to be a bird of some kind, right?" Arnold pressed.

"Possibly. Some people are said to have vivid dreams of embodying their spirit beasts before they manifest. You also know that bird spirit beasts are quite rare. Try not to rush this, son. When your body is ready, it will happen. I can assure you of that."

A strange expression came across Bernard's face, as if there was something more he wanted to say. "You are going to go through changes. You may become quicker or stronger or have better reflexes, and all that is going to depend on the spirit beast that you have inside of you. If you have a strong enough connection to your spirit beast, you may be able to summon it one day as I can, but it is not the be-all and end-all." Bernard took another bite of his toast, leaving a trail of crumbs on the table.

"I need one if I am to be a Doyen like you," Arnold said. He couldn't help but feel disappointed. This is what Arnold wanted more than anything, a career with the Spirit Wardens, protecting people. Doyen was a rank given to protectors within the Spirit Wardens and it was no easy feat to get it. Doyens were tasked with keeping the villages, towns, and cities where they were posted safe from those who chose to misuse the powers they had been gifted via their spirit beasts. That said, recently it had become more likely that those without a connection were the ones more likely to cause trouble. Arnold's dad had dedicated his life to training to harness his powers in order to become a Doyen, having come from a long line of Doyens and Elders. Arnold never doubted for one second that he himself would join as soon as he turned eighteen.

"You're nearly fifteen now, so before long you will know exactly what your spirit beast is. As I said, don't rush it. You can't join the Spirit Wardens and become a Doyen for a good few years, so for the time being, go and enjoy being a kid," Bernard said, frowning at Arnold. "Trust me when I say that being a Doyen is not as exciting as you think; it is not all action. There is a lot of training, both physical and mental, that you need to endure."

Bernard looked across the table at his son's slightly crestfallen face and smiled gently. "I know you want to know what your spirit beast is, and that's completely normal at your age." He took another bite of his toast, which made a loud crunch as he bit down, forcing some of the marmalade to push up against his dark, greying moustache. Arnold mustered a smile at this and nodded at his dad to indicate he had marmalade on his face. Bernard quickly brushed it off before he picked up his newspaper and began reading again.

As Bernard finished his toast off, there was a brisk knock at the door, one that Arnold instantly recognised.

"That will be Otto, Arnold," Eve called from the kitchen. "Time to head for school." Arnold stood up to leave the breakfast table. As he rose to his feet, he collided with the corner of the table, letting out a frustrated sigh. Not only was he still unsure of his spirit beast, but he also struggled with the awkwardness of his adolescent growth, with gangly limbs that did nothing to boost his self-image. He grabbed his bag and coat from the hook in the hallway as Eve handed him his lunchbox.

Arnold's best friend Otto Redburn was waiting for him outside.

"Orite," Otto greeted Arnold in his thick northern accent. Otto was of a stronger build than Arnold, with an athletic stature, broad shoulders, and olive-toned skin that made Arnold feel as though he resembled a ghost in comparison.

Otto was also slightly taller, but Arnold assured himself that this was only because Otto was a few months older. Much to Arnold's jealousy, Otto's spirit beast had begun to manifest itself already. It was still in the early stages, but Otto's athleticism had improved since his fifteenth birthday, and his shoulders had grown broader, so much so that his shirt threatened to pop its buttons should he continue to grow at this rate. The Redburn family had a history of their spirit beasts being those of the big cats. Otto's dad's was a lynx and his grandad's was a snow leopard, so Otto believed his spirit beast was going to be pretty epic.

"Morning, Otoronco," Bernard called from inside.

Otto rolled his eyes and laughed to Arnold, shaking his head to clear his slightly long, brown tangled hair from his face. "Please just call me Otto, Mr. Ethon," he said, his thick accent suddenly sounding well-spoken like he had been rehearsing these lines. Otto often had to ask people to refer to him by his shortened name, and Arnold knew he was uncomfortable trying to live up to the legacy of his great-grandad, whom he was named after.

"I don't think your mum and dad would appreciate that!" Bernard's laugh could be heard from the dining room as he walked out and waved in Otto's direction. "Please say hi to them from me, and let your dad know I am ready for that round of golf whenever he is. Or is he too busy now that he's mayor?"

"I'm sure he could use the break," Otto replied, "he's a bit obsessed with trying to get the coal mines re-opened at the moment."

"Oh, that's right," Bernard said, nodding. "I wish your dad luck. That would certainly bring in some much-needed cash flow into the town."

"Dad, we're going to be late!" Arnold said, not wanting to give his dad the chance to embark on one of his monologues about the economic state of Oswaldtwistle.

During Oswaldtwistle's coal-mine era, Otto's great-grandad had worked his way up from being in the mines all day to eventually being a foreman. Otto's family still resided in the old foreman's house, which was the largest of the terraced houses that sat in the middle of his street, to this day.

This had been handed down from his great-grandad and then down to his dad and now he lived there with his parents and his five-year-old brother, Taron.

Arnold shouted goodbye to his parents and set off down the road towards the school with Otto. It was quiet outside, and the sun was slowly rising, the sky still a greyish pale colour. The birds could be heard singing their morning songs, and a gentle breeze was in the air, just enough to ensure that a coat was needed. The ground was wet with the overnight showers; small puddles littered the road and pavements, just waiting for an over-zealous car driver to drive through and soak them.

"You decided what you want to do for your birthday?" Otto asked, hopscotching around the puddles with enviable agility. Arnold felt certain his spirit beast would be something feline. The Redburns were known as Agnates – their spirit beasts were linked through family blood, a rare phenomenon, so it was likely that Otto would take after his ancestors.

As for his birthday, Arnold didn't have a large circle of friends, meaning a party was out of the question.

"Maybe just head to the cinema?" he replied, looking at Otto for assurances that this was a promising idea. There were a couple of films that had come out recently that he would like to see.

"Sounds good."

Arnold and Otto continued their usual walk to school across the sports field and through an alleyway that led past the local Spirit Wardens headquarters, where Arnold's dad worked. It was also where the local Doyens – those tasked with keeping the town safe – were based. This was where the Doyens honed their skills through training and learned to truly master their inner spirit beasts, with access to a library full of literature about the ancient ways.

The building's shape was similar to the pyramids of Egypt, except the steep incline was layered with steps leading to the top, rather than a traditional smooth finish. At the top of these steps sat the entranceway, a rectangular extension built from large blocks of limestone and carved into shape. The steps of the Spirit Wardens were inlaid with carved hieroglyphs denoting the spirit beasts of fallen Doyens or Elders. It was considered the highest honour for those serving the Spirit Wardens to have their legacies carved here, but one that no man or woman ever lived to witness for this was only awarded upon death.

"One day, my spirit beast is going to be etched into this building," Arnold said, making the statement with a sense of steely pride as he gazed up at it. The bright sky behind the building made the grey stone shine as if a sheet of glass covered it, making it seem even more impressive. He wanted to be a Doyen so badly; it was all Arnold thought about lately even though it was still over three years before he would be old enough to join.

"Not like you to mention that," Otto teased.

"Well, it will be."

"Don't you think you need to have a spirit beast before you can join? You haven't even begun to show signs of your spirit beast yet, so let's face it, Arnold – you're some way off from becoming a Doyen." Otto chuckled to himself, oblivious to any offence he might have caused.

"Wow – don't hold back," Arnold replied, Otto's comments irritating him. He was completely right, though. Arnold put his hands in his pockets and kicked out at a small stone which skimmed across the pavement, the loud clicks echoing as it bounced off the floor before coming to a stop on the other side of the road.

"Sometimes, you need to be realistic with these things," Otto continued, a playful grin across his face. "Come on, we are going to be late if you stand here daydreaming all day." He looked at his watch. "Mr. Higgins will kill me if I'm late to form once more. Last one there is a menial!" he said playfully.

Otto set off running up the street at speed, hurdling past the puddles with ease. He even vaulted a wall with minimal effort as he took a shortcut to get to school on time. Arnold couldn't help but laugh to himself. For someone so quick, Otto was always late or arrived at the last minute, something he was on report for at school. Though Arnold was happy for Otto, he couldn't help but feel a little bit jealous that he had started showing physical signs of his spirit beast, something Arnold was still anxiously waiting to experience.

Arnold set off running after Otto, but it felt like an age to catch up to him as he was so much quicker. Arnold wasn't even a fraction as agile, so he couldn't vault over the wall like his friend had, choosing to run around it instead.

Legs burning and chest heaving, Arnold finally caught up to Otto, who was leaning smugly against the entrance gates to the school.

"Yeah, coz that was a fair race!" Arnold puffed as he caught his breath.

Otto smirked. "Don't be so bitter! You never know, you might beat me one day."

"The sooner the better," Arnold laughed. "You're becoming unbearable!"

Until his gifts finally started to manifest, all Arnold had to look forward to were his dreams, and he couldn't wait to go to sleep again so that he could enjoy the sensation of flying once more.

# CHAPTER 2

"I had another dream that I was flying last night," Arnold told Otto as the two of them walked through the compacted hallways of school. "It felt so real, I could honestly feel the cold air against me."

"I'm guessing you left a window open."

Arnold shook his head slowly at Otto's continued attempt to wind him up.

"I'm all ears." Otto raised his eyebrows, apparently realising that he had just about got away with that last joke at Arnold's expense.

Arnold and Otto continued their walk towards their forms to register for the day through the hustle and bustle of varying groups walking and talking as they recounted weekend activities.

Arnold was so focused on his conversation with Otto that he did not notice the group standing at the side of the corridor in front of him. With a thud, Arnold clattered his shoulder into one of them completely by accident, knocking him sideways.

"Ethon! Watch where you're going!" The boy turned around, his cheeks scarlet, though whether from embarrassment or rage, Arnold wasn't sure. His heart sank when he realised who it was: Kaden Aspis. Kaden was the most popular boy in school, with thick blond hair, bright green eyes tinged with yellow, and a strong athletic build. As captain of the football team, Kaden was popular as he was arrogant.

"Sorry, Kaden." Arnold lowered his head, cheeks burning. The activity in the moving corridor seemed to suddenly stop as all eyes were on him, like a cascading river hitting a dam.

"What was that?" Kaden asked, slamming his hand into Arnold's shoulder. "You're going to need to speak louder than that." Behind him, Arnold spotted the smug, sneering faces of Piers Lepus and Caleb Muridae. The two of them followed Kaden everywhere and did everything they were told. Also powerfully built, Piers had long dark hair tied back and was the goalkeeper for the football team, while Caleb resembled a rat in Arnold's eyes, with his pointed nose and buckteeth. Arnold knew that Kaden only accepted him because his parents were rich, and he was a great winger for the squad.

Arnold raised his head to meet Kaden's dominating stare. "I said I'm sorry, I didn't mean to –"

Before Arnold had chance to say another word, Kaden pushed Arnold towards the wall, dropping his bag on the floor so his hands were free to grab Arnold. As Kaden gripped Arnold by the scruff of his blazer, Arnold could feel the power in his arms and he braced himself for a thump, wincing in anticipation.

Otto quickly stepped in, however, knocking away Kaden's hands and breaking his grasp. "Move on, Kaden," he said sternly, "Arnold said he was sorry."

The two of them stood nose to nose for a moment, electricity dancing in the air around them both. Piers and Caleb stepped forward, readying for a fight, and Arnold's heart sank. He had never had a fight before and did not want his first one to be against the three toughest and most popular boys in their year.

"Wow, you really can smell the macho boys here, can't you?" The voice came from Everett Harris, a girl who Arnold knew from a couple of his classes but had never spoken to before. She had dark skin and long curls of black hair, her eyes an entrancing, icy blue. The world seemed to move in slow motion as she swaggered past, her best friend Georgina Vulpine by her side.

"Boys will be boys," said George sarcastically.

"Keep your nose out," Kaden sniped. "This doesn't involve you."

Unfazed by her ex-boyfriend, Everett paused for a moment as if she might intervene on Arnold's behalf. Instead, she raised her hand dismissively and continued to class, disappearing out of sight.

Kaden's attention returned to Arnold, Otto still standing unflinching in between the two of them. "Cross my path again, Ethon, and I will destroy you!" he said through gritted teeth.

Arnold didn't know what to do, so he simply nodded his head submissively.

"You will have to get through me first," Otto huffed, his gaze firmly fixed on Kaden.

Kaden stared back for a moment before smiling and straightening his blazer. "Come on, boys, I can't be late to register again. I'll be stopped from playing football if I am put on report." He held out his hand and Piers passed him his school bag which he threw over his shoulder. "Until next time, Ethon." He smiled and the three of them set off down the corridor, leaving Arnold standing there hoping that the ground would swallow him up.

"Not the brightest idea you have had, mate," Otto said, straightening up his ruffled collar and school tie.

Arnold sighed. "Thanks for stepping in. I dread to think what would have happened if you weren't here."

"Don't see them picking on anyone that's connected with their spirit beasts. They're cowards if you ask me."

"Come on, we best hurry up, we don't want to be late," Arnold said, surveying the hall. No one seemed to be looking at him anymore, but that did not seem to stem the heat that had flashed into his cheeks.

ARNOLD MADE it through the first half of the day without any more drama, somehow surviving the boredom that came with Monday's lessons. He didn't have any classes with Kaden and the others, but knew he had a full week to get through before the weekend. Hopefully he could just keep his head down and keep out of Kaden's way.

As school days went, it was up there with the more boring ones. Maths followed by physics made this morning an extra special mind-numbing one for Arnold. He didn't pay attention in maths, and instead spent the lesson colouring in the alternative squares that filled his math book rather than doing the revision the class had been requested to do.

Arnold felt as though his mind was going into a dark hole as he etched his pencil into the small squares, making a small scratching noise in the process. All he could think about was his vivid, recurring dream, the sensation of flying, and how real it felt. He wanted this to be a sign of his spirit beast so badly, it was all he could think about. He started colouring in the squares faster and faster, pressing down harder until eventually the end of his pencil broke, snapping Arnold's attention back into the room.

"Have you worked out your frustration, Ethon?" the substitute teacher asked, drawing attention to the fact he wasn't doing the revision that he had been asked to do. Arnold had been oblivious to how frantically he had been scribbling in his book.

Leaning across the rectangular table, Arnold opened up the thick maths book and began to take notes on algebra.

"This is pointless." The mutter came out of his mouth without him even realising it.

"Pardon?"

There was a snigger in the room coming from some of Arnold's classmates, surprised by his outburst. This was most unlike him.

"Nothing, sir." He began silently working on his revision notes, not that any of it was sinking in as again all he could think about was his spirit beast and what it would be. He'd struggle with these lessons on a normal day, but today, his dream was taking up all the mind space that he had.

He knew it was only a matter of time before his spirit beast manifested but he was beginning to grow frustrated at waiting for a physical sign. He wanted the changes to happen to him now and scribbling notes about algebra was not going to help.

Maths finished and after packing up his things, he left the class and set off down the corridor to the science block. The corridors were narrow and avoiding bumping into other students was a hard task in itself. The noise of students talking to each other about what they had been up to at the weekend filled the space, and just from walking from maths to science, Arnold managed to catch up on all the recent gossip without muttering a word.

Kacy Grange and Caleb Stead had broken up for the fifteenth time, Barry Winks had gotten drunk at Henrietta Winslow's party and been sick in her mum's wardrobe, and the juiciest of all was that Mr. Ebbs and Miss Reah from the science department had been seen out together holding hands.

Arnold was happy keeping to himself at school, especially after how the morning had started. He didn't have the largest group of friends. In fact, his only real friend was Otto, and he was quite happy with that. They'd bonded three years ago over their shared interests in comics and superheroes, and they'd stuck together ever since.

After what felt like the longest of eternities, Arnold had made it through the two horrifically boring lessons and it was finally lunch time. He soon found himself sat at one of the benches in the dinner hall making his way through the ham and cheese sandwiches that his mum had made for him. He was so engrossed in thoughts about his dream that the noisy hustle and bustle of dinner time in the hall felt like white noise. He was aware of it but didn't pay any attention to it. Otto came and joined him at the table, sitting opposite him with a daft grin drawn across his face. He was looking across at Arnold as if he was waiting to be prompted on what he was thinking. Arnold did not say a word, waiting for his friend to speak.

"Maybe you're a bat," Otto spurted out excitedly, unable to contain his theory any longer. It seemed as though Arnold wasn't the only one who had spent the morning contemplating what his dreams could symbolise.

Arnold had just taken a huge gulp of his orange juice, which he had to stop himself spitting out across the table. He took a moment to gather himself. "I don't think so, Otto. The way I am flying in my dreams is as though I'm gliding. The way bats fly is scatty and erratic. It wouldn't make sense to be a bat." He let out a sigh as he finished his sandwich before helping it down with another big gulp of juice. "I just wish that my spirit beast would give me some sort of sign and not just in a dream. I mean, why can't anything be happening to me like it is you?" Arnold couldn't help but feel guilty from the wave of frustration coming over him, making it seem as though he was mad at his friend. If his jealousy was spilling out, he needed to get a better grip on his feelings and not let his frustrations consume him.

"It will happen, mate, don't worry," Otto said.

"What does it feel like? When you start to get that connection?"

"It's hard to explain, but when it does manifest, it just kind of happens. You don't have any control over it. It's a bit like something is tugging at your stomach from the inside. Remember, I haven't fully connected with mine yet, so you might be best asking someone else."

A loud crash startled Arnold from across the hall. It sounded as though a metal tray had been dropped and Arnold waited for the usual sarcastic cheer to engulf the hall which was usually the case when someone had done this. However, this did not happen, and he looked across the hall where there appeared to be some sort of commotion. He could hear the whispers from the other school kids that formed a large circle around something, which slowly turned into chanting and laughter. Arnold half expected a fight to have broken out, but again he was wrong.

The younger kids began to run away from the gathering students, while the older kids moved towards the disturbance. Otto and Arnold gave each other looks before nodding in silent, almost telepathic agreement, then followed suite and ran across the hall, pushing their way through the large crowd. When they found themselves at the front of the throng of students, Arnold's mouth fell open.

"Bloody hell," Otto said.

Everett was standing there with a look of bewilderment, excitement, and embarrassment. Her ice-blue eyes looked intense against her dark skin, her gaze fixed firmly on what was in front of her.

Otto had often joked that Everett's spirit beast would turn out to be a bull due to her notorious bull-in-a-China-shop attitude, but he'd been wrong. Standing there in front of Everett on the table was a small boar, which had manifested for the first time and completely out of the blue judging by the panicked expression on Everett's face.

"Well, that's a little embarrassing," Otto mumbled. "At least I was kind of right."

A soft, purple glow emitted from the beast as it began knocking everything off the table, sending dishes and lunches flying as it kicked out in a panicked state.

Arnold could tell it was a boar by the two small tusks protruding from its mouth underneath its large, round snout. The boar was sniffing out loudly, nuzzling its snout on the table clearly over-stimulated by the different smells emitting from the food in the dinner hall. Arnold could not believe his eyes. He had never seen someone summon a spirit beast for the first time, and he found himself analysing every part of it, wanting to absorb as much as he could before the boar vanished again. More than anything, he wanted to be as ready and prepared as he could for when it finally happened to him.

"It's rude to stare," Everett snapped at the group that had formed, blushing with the embarrassment at what was happening.

Arnold couldn't help but feel sorry for her, given the current situation. This was the first time Everett had summoned her spirit beast and she had done it by accident in front of everyone.

The boar shook its body, starting from its head and moving all the way down to its short tail, padding its feet on the floor.

"It's going to charge!" a voice called out from the crowd.

The spirit beast ran at a full sprint down the table, knocking all the lunches that were on it into the air, spilling everything all over the floor. There was a combination of screams and nervous laughter from the other students as the boar hurtled down the hall to the other side, running underneath the tables and bumping into the legs, causing the lunches that were atop to also come crashing to the ground.

"I don't know what to do, what do I do now?" Everett spoke with confusion, hoping anyone in the hall would help. "Why is it behaving like this?"

"How do you expect us to know?" laughed Otto. "Clearly, we are lacking in the spirit beast department. Why not try stopping it trashing the hall first, eh? Might be a good start."

"It's reacting to you," Arnold said. "It's connected to you, remember? It feels what you feel."

Everett gave Arnold a hard stare. "Meaning?"

"It will respond to your emotions."

"Well, don't just stand there gawping, help me!" she snapped, a look of panicked desperation on her face.

The poor girl looked absolutely mortified at the situation. They couldn't let her do this on her own. Arnold knew they needed to help her as it was the right thing to do. After all, this could have happened to anyone, and Arnold liked to think that someone would help him if he stood in Everett's shoes. It wasn't uncommon for someone's first time to happen in front of others and the last thing Arnold would want would be for loads of people to be gawping at him.

"What's the matter, Everett? Can't get your beast under control? Think it's a perfect fit for you!" Kaden shouted, a chorus of laughter joining his heckles.

Everett's focus turned to Kaden, her expression turning from embarrassment to fury. Kaden continued to laugh smugly with his friends until they pointed out to him that Everett's spirit beast was firmly fixed on him.

With a squeal, the boar let out its newly found battle cry and charged at Kaden, whose laughter quickly turned to panic. For a moment his eyes widened, and a yellow glow surrounded him as if he was ready and willing to summon his own spirit beast to defend himself, but before he had time, the boar hurled itself through the air, sending Kaden clattering into Piers and Caleb. The rest of the pupils surrounding them were sent sprawling across the floor like skittles hit by a bowling ball.

The boar shook its head, dazed by the attack. Sensing an opportunity, Arnold dove for the boar, but it was quicker than him and darted out of the way before charging back down the dinner hall.

Cries and screams rang out as those watching did not want to stick around to see if the boar would attack them next. Students clambered over one another as they pushed and pulled to get out the exit door first.

Everett and Otto set off chasing the boar around the hall, trying their hardest to catch it, but they seemed to only antagonise it further as it continued to kick out sporadically and shake its head around aggressively. It charged at Otto, seemingly unimpressed at his attempts to stop it, clattering straight into his legs and sending him crashing over a table. A loud thud could be heard followed by a yelp as he hit the floor and a tray of food landed on top of him. Otto's cheeks reddened as laughter broke out around him.

"Everett, get control of it!" he snapped.

"I am trying!"

"You need to settle it, Everett!" Arnold shouted across the hall. He knew a lot about spirit beasts thanks to his obsession with them, having done lots of reading and research on how they worked.

"You need to calm yourself, first. Try to relax and that should reassure it. It's just as panicked as you are." Arnold wanted to help as best he could. "Remember, it is connected to you, to your emotions." He ran back across the hall to help Otto to his feet, pulling him up and brushing away the sandwich fillings that were on his blazer.

Everett looked unsure but began to try and gather herself before shrugging her shoulders and walking steadily towards her spirit beast, which had backed itself into a corner. Slowly,

Everett made her way towards the spectral boar and placed her hand out towards it. The purple glow around the boar drifted towards Everett's hand. Although her hand was shaking, she was able to place it on the animal's back. Her contact with the boar appeared to calm it, and it turned its head and nuzzled into Everett's palm, making a soft grunting noise. A rare smile came across Everett's face and Arnold could not help but think how pretty she looked as her spirit beast began to dissipate and absorb back into her.

"I can't believe it!" Arnold was so happy to see a spirit beast so up-close.

"Tell me about it," Otto agreed. He paused for a second before continuing. "Everett smiled."

Arnold gave Otto a slight dig in his ribs with his elbow.

"Ow, what did you do that for?"

The large double doors to the dining hall swung open and Miss Elstone walked in, looking aghast at the state of the hall. She was a short, plump woman with grey hair that was tied back into a bun on the top of her head. She had her hands placed firmly on her hips, her bright orange cardigan distracting Arnold from the frustration etched across her face.

"Everybody out!" she bellowed, and just like she had cast a spell, everyone left in the dinner hall began to leave. "Except you three." She signalled across the hall at Everett, Otto, and Arnold, who stopped in their tracks. "You three will spend the rest of the day cleaning this mess up."

"But we –" Otto began to argue their case but he was quickly shot down by Miss Elstone who simply raised her hand to gesture for him to shut up.

"Miss Harris, you are not the first to have the misfortune of this happening in a public place and you will not be the last. However, there is a mess in the hall that needs cleaning and as it was your spirit beast, I am afraid you will have to take responsibility." Her tone was serious, her face stony and rigid. "I suggest you learn to control your emotions sooner rather than later. Master Ethon, Master Redburn, as you seemed so eager to chase her spirit beast around the hall and antagonise it, you can also help."

Arnold felt hard done by his punishment. After all, they were only trying to help Everett, but there was no winning over Miss Elstone; the deputy head teacher was renowned as a strict disciplinarian whom most found intimidating and did not dare cross.

The three of them knew that they would not get anywhere by protesting, so they set off cleaning the large dining hall, which suddenly seemed much bigger with just the three of them in it.

Plate glass windows that had not been replaced since the '70s lined the perimeter, ensuring that just enough natural light filled the hall without the need to switch the lights on. The clanging of trays echoed from Otto making a point that he was not happy about his task. Arnold set to work mopping the floor, the combination of cheap bleach and other cleaning products giving the mixture a lemon smell which was slightly overpowering. There was that much stuff on the floor that he was needing to change the water several times whilst he made his way across the room.

"This is torture, Arnold, worse than prison." Carrying more trays than he should, Otto walked across the room to the kitchen door, mumbling to himself. There was a loud clatter as he dropped the plates onto the floor due to carrying too many. Arnold and Everett set about laughing together as Otto cursed to himself.

The two of them got into a good system, with Everett sweeping the food off the floor while Arnold mopped up behind her. Looking at what they had managed to do, he felt that they should be done before their final period was finished, meaning they shouldn't be getting any detentions. Not today, anyway.

Everett put her brush to one side and stopped for a short rest. "I just want to say thank you for helping me," she said. "Everyone else was too busy staring and laughing at me."

"Wow, an acknowledgement. Not like you, Everett," Otto called from beyond the hatch.

"Funny, forget what I said then," she snapped back.

Arnold rolled his eyes. "Ignore him. That's what I do." He felt his cheeks start to give off a soft glow from her thanking him. He quickly turned away so that Everett wouldn't notice. "What did it feel like?" he asked.

"Erm, embarrassing." Everett looked taken aback by the question. She let down her black hair to re-tie it with a bobble before setting off sweeping the floor again.

"Not the situation. I mean, how did it feel summoning your spirit beast, what was it like?" Arnold continued to shuffle along the floor, mopping away the trail of destruction that had been left by the very spirit beast he was asking about.

"Really strange, if I'm honest. I had a strange sensation in my stomach, a sickly kind of feeling. I remember feeling annoyed that some boy had just jumped in the chair I was about to sit on and before I knew it, it was stood there and I was freaking out. I can't believe that out of all the spirit beasts, I have a boar."

"A boar is pretty cool if you ask me."

"Really? I haven't got a clue what it means. I'll have to speak to my dad when I get home to find out more about it."

Arnold thought back to some of what he'd learned during his quest to figure out what his own spirit beast might be. "Pig-like spirit beasts are deemed to be some of the most intelligent, which most people don't realise. Boars are considered to be more wild than pigs but are renowned for their courage as well as their overall fierceness." He reeled off facts as if reading from a Wikipedia page. "At least, I think that's what it is. I think that it complements you really well."

"Thanks." There was a short pause from Everett. "I guess," she mumbled, as if not really sure how to take Arnold's comments.

Out of nowhere, Otto jumped into the conversation and said, "It's Arnold's birthday at the weekend, fancy coming to the cinemas with us?"

"Otto!" Arnold could have killed him, diving in like that. He felt his face beginning to get warm as his cheeks blushed again, giving him a complex.

"Sure, why not? I've nothing else planned. Don't be getting any ideas though, boys."

Otto gave Arnold a cheeky wink. "You can thank me later," he muttered under his breath. Arnold didn't think it was that obvious that he fancied Everett, but if Otto had realised it, it must have been.

The three of them spent the remainder of the school day cleaning and managed to get this done before the day was out. A new friendship had begun to develop and Arnold couldn't help but feel his circle of friends had just gotten a little bit larger. Combined with seeing a spirit beast so up-close, today had turned into a good day.

# CHAPTER 3

Sat in a chair in a quaint little flat, an elderly man was drinking tea out of an old bone China tea set, gazing out the window and watching the world go by. He could see part of his reflection through the window, and he wasn't the strapping young man he used to be. A weary face that looked as though it had experienced a lot of pain stared back at him. He had always blamed his busy work life from years past and the stresses that came with his job for the wrinkles that tracked across his forehead.

The sound of two clocks ticking in the background could be heard, though not in tandem with each other which would drive most people stir-crazy. But for this old boy, he had become acquainted to the noise, to the point where he hardly noticed the ticking at all. Placing his teacup on the table with a soft clinking noise, the man picked up the teapot and filled his cup once more, letting out a small sigh of appreciation. He did like a nice pot of tea, after all.

The small flat felt cluttered with all his personal treasures and mementos from his eventful life and career, which filled the glass cabinet and every inch of spare surface in the room, from on top of the fire to sections of the dining table. On the walls were pictures of a younger version of himself with friends from years ago from different expeditions all over the world.

Stood next to him in one photo was a beautiful red-haired lady with enchanting green eyes, the colour resembling that of a sparkling emerald as the light had caught them. The photos on the wall eventually came to photos of this enchantingly beautiful woman and himself on various dates from bowling to the outdoor cinema before coming to photos of their wedding day, and what a magical day that was.

He often thought fondly of these moments that he had shared with his wife. Looking back brought him nothing but happiness with only a few regrets, which was why there were so many photographs scattered around the room with varying mismatched frames. His own personal museum of his extraordinary life.

He felt an emptiness inside now, brought on by the unbearable grief of his wife's passing two years ago. She was the person he had shared everything with. Her death had left him alone in life, giving him a sense of bitterness towards fate. He often wished that it had been him who'd been taken by the chest condition that had plagued his wife in her later years and had cruelly stolen her life.

She balanced his personality and had brought out the better side of him. Without her, he was now a lonely, bitter man who had become a recluse to the local community, uninterested in most things. He simply had no interest in the world now, as it was so much duller without his beloved wife. After a marriage that had spanned forty years, the fact of the matter was that he simply did not know what to do with himself now he was alone. He had no friends anymore, a consequence of his own isolation paired with the icy touch of death catching up with them in their old age.

Looking at the small, old-fashioned clock that sat at the centre of the table where he sat drinking his tea, the man noticed the time and felt that he best set off to complete his tasks for the day in town which consisted of collecting some items from the shop for his evening meal, and maybe going to the local bookies to place a couple of pounds worth of bets on the football match. Short trips into town were about the most adventurous he got nowadays, as he opted to spend the majority of his time either reading or watching television in the comfort of his home. He had found that since his wife's passing, he no longer had much tolerance for other people and hated the idle pleasantries of creating fake conversation just to fit the social expectations of everyone. He had no time for this. He'd much rather get out into town to do what he needed to do and return to the comforts of his flat where no one could bother him.

He finished off his cup of tea before putting on his shoes, coat, and flat cap, then gingerly walked down the steps of his small flat to the front door. As he leaned slightly towards the wall to keep his balance, the handrail wobbled beneath his weight. He hated these stairs and the difficulties they created for him, but he didn't want to move, as he had shared this flat with his beloved and he was too proud – or stubborn, as his wife would have called it – to ask for help by way of having a stair lift put in.

The old man locked his front door and hobbled down the cobbled path through his well-maintained garden before turning and heading down the road towards his local supermarket. Maybe he would treat himself to a bottle of his favourite red wine this evening. It was Saturday, after all.

The weather report had forecasted intermittent showers throughout the day and for this reason he did not want to be out too long. The weather was looking slightly overcast with the sun trying to burn its way through the greying clouds.

Making it to the supermarket, he slowly wandered around the maze-like aisles collecting the items he needed for tea. The floor looked like it had been buffered to within an inch of its existence, creating a shine that he had only ever seen at a bowling alley. He couldn't help but wonder how people his age were expected to walk on the highly polished surface without slipping. He edged around the increasingly dangerous environment with even more care, this latest obstacle joining the long lists of hazards he now faced daily.

When he had finished collecting his items, he made his way to the checkout area using the small trolley he had acquired to keep himself balanced. The young checkout assistant scanned his items and gave him a smile to which he didn't respond. He packed the items into the long-life bag he'd brought with him to avoid buying another plastic carrier, then headed to his local bookmakers to place a bet on the football this afternoon. He opted for three different variations of a fivefold accumulator for this afternoon's matches. He was feeling lucky.

Managing to avoid most conversation, he left the bookmakers, looked up at the sky, and decided he best head back to his flat, as the clouds had gotten darker and looked as though the heavens were about to open on him.

He briefly contemplated going back into the bookmakers and asking for them to ring a taxi for him but decided against this, as he did not want to waste money when he didn't live that far away. A little down the road, he regretted that decision when the weather turned and it started to rain heavily. He couldn't help but regret his own stubbornness on this occasion.

The rain bounced from the pavement as a steady wind began to pick up. The sudden change in the weather surprised him, as only a light shower had been forecasted.

The storm was unforgiving. Rain lashed his strained face as the wind worked against him. Within moments he was drenched to the bone. He may as well have jumped in a swimming pool for how wet he was. The man stopped for a moment to assess which route would be the best to get back to the warmth of his home as quickly as possible. He squinted his eyes, looking across the increasingly flooded football field that sat in between him and his house.

He normally avoided the pathway down the side of the field, preferring to walk all the way around in order to dodge the local youths who tended to hang around. But the rain was now coming down even heavier, and unable to see anyone congregated on this route, he decided that today, he would take the narrow footpath. Trudging down along the path, he attempted to avoid the puddles that had quickly formed, as he didn't feel like spoiling his new shoes that he had only purchased recently. Deep down, he already knew that they'd be damaged by the torrential downpour. Why had he bothered coming out? If he had known the weather was going to be like this, he would have jumped in a taxi, and he was cursing the fact that he hadn't.

"Charles Grey!" a deep, gravelly voice boomed from behind him. The man did not say his name like you would if you thought you recognised a friend.

Stopping in his tracks, Charles felt a shudder down his spine along with a sudden spike in adrenaline as his heart began to race. A sense of dread came over him as he turned around.

The rain made it difficult for his already deteriorating eyesight to make out any details of the speaker. Standing there was a tall, powerfully built man wearing a long, black overcoat. Rain cascaded down his jacket to his clenched fists. The stranger's face was marked with three symmetrical scars down one side of his face, making him look even more sinister.

The man smiled. "Charles Grey!" he bellowed once more. "I have been looking for you for some time. It has taken a while, but here you are. I can sense you, I can sense it. You have been here all along."

Charles could see that this stranger was furious at him. The aggression in his voice was frightening as he shouted.

Startled, Charles stepped back. This man knew who he was, or what he used to do, what he used to be. How could this be, though? He had kept to himself since retiring and there were only a handful of people around that knew him personally and professionally. Charles had happily lived a quiet life in his older years as a means to keep himself and his late wife safe.

"I have no idea what you mean." The words stuttered out of his mouth with little confidence.

"Don't take me for a fool," the stranger sneer, a twisted smile overcoming his shadow-laden face. He pulled his jacket to the side, revealing something that reflected what little light there was.

Charles squinted, initially unable to make out what it was, but when the stranger reached inside his jacket and removed the item, his heart sank.

The hilt of the weapon was made with polished black stone, with intricate carvings decorating the side of it. The blade looked as though it was made from bone.

Charles recoiled in horror at what he was seeing, and for a moment, he froze. "It can't be!" he murmured to himself. He was almost certain that he recognised the blade, and instantly understood what this man was here to do. His mouth instantly became dry as his entire body began to tremble. He was too old, too frail to try and outrun the man. He himself was unarmed, apart from the small shopping bag in his hand.

Charles surveyed his surroundings, trying to come up with some sort of plan. He gripped the bag tightly, realising there was no easy way out of this situation. He would fight if he had to.

Before he knew it, the attacker ran at him with speed far superior than anything Charles had ever seen. The man swung the blade back and aimed a strike at Charles, the blade glistening unnaturally in the rain.

Charles heaved the bag he was carrying and slammed it into the side of the man's head, then, diving out of the way of the blade, he rolled to try and gain some distance between himself and his attacker, showing the agility of someone in prime fitness and not that of an elderly man.

The stranger scowled. "I knew it was you." A crooked smile overcame his face, his lip bleeding from the blow. He ran at Charles again, this time aiming a kick which made contact with him as he lay on the floor. The force sent Charles rolling on his side through the water puddling on the field.

Gasping for breath and heavily winded by the strike, Charles attempted to pick himself up from the floor, his hands sliding through heavy mud that had formed beneath him.

He attempted to pick himself up, but his arms buckled and he fell back to the ground. Rolling onto his back, he lay there with his chest convulsing as he attempted to regain his breath, his clothes sticking to him tightly as he became covered in rain and mud.

He was alone. No one was coming to help him. He couldn't help but wonder if anyone would notice when he was gone. The intense feeling of sadness overcame him as he lay there knowing that this was it, that his time was up. He took comfort in the knowledge that he would soon be reunited with his wife.

Within seconds of thinking of his wife, he had a feeling in the pit of his stomach, one he had not experienced for a long time. His body began to emit a soft yellow glow and suddenly a warm sensation came over him. His breathing steadied itself and his chest no longer throbbed where he had been struck. He felt calmer. Knowing he did not have time to dwell on the situation, Charles began to climb to his knees as if being guided by strings. It was pulling him to his feet, it wanted him to get up and fight back. Managing to get to one knee, he planted his other foot firmly on the mud-covered floor, ready to stand up and prepare himself should the man strike him again.

He felt rejuvenated, as if he was in his prime again, and it was a good feeling. A feeling that had been a long time coming. It was as though a deep fog that was in his mind had instantly dissipated and the path he needed to walk was now clear.

As the rain continued to hammer the two of them, the scarred man walked over to Charles and swung his blade towards him with incredible force.

Knowing he was not done for yet, Charles raised his hands above his head and grabbed the hilt of the blade as well as his attacker's hands before pushing him away with equal force, as though he had turned his attacker's strength against him.

Charles caught a better glimpse of the blade, all but confirming his suspicions. And if he was right, the weapon was extremely dangerous, especially if this stranger knew what it was capable of.

The stranger steadied himself from being pushed backwards and grinned at Charles again. His mouth was thin and curt, and he was now looking even more sinister than before. He didn't seem surprised by Charles's strength.

"That's a good start, Charles. Now show it to me. I want to see it," the man snarled.

Charles was feeling energised, but he knew the kick he'd received had broken a rib, and once his auro faded, he would feel the pain to its fullest extent.

He knew he had no option but to cave to the scarred man's demands if he was to survive this night. He desperately hoped that he still had his lifelong companion within him after all this time.

Raising his hands in the air, Charles began to move them around in a figure-eight-like motion, the yellow glow from his auro leaving a light trail behind his hands, allowing the shape he was forming to light up the air around him. His hands moving faster and faster, Charles began to feel the sensation of something rising up within him. He had forgotten how this felt, and he held back a wave of nausea that overcame him to continue the process.

The attacker remained still, his horrifically disfigured face lit up from the yellow glow that Charles was emitting, intrigued by what he was seeing and excited by what was about to happen. He tightened the grip on his blade, biding his time before his next move, the rain still pouring down his heavily scarred face.

A bright flash of light lit up the field. In front of Charles, his spirit beast began to form. Charles continued to motion his hands in the air and concentrated on his beast taking its form. He had not done this in years and hoped that he would not fail, knowing that if he did, his time would be up. Letting out a cry of anger and frustration at the attacker, Charles finished motioning his hands, the sound of his shouts overtaken by the deafening roar of his spirit beast, which was now stood in front of him in its powerful form of a hippo.

The spectral hippo looked battle-worn, its thick, grey skin cracked from the many battles it had experienced in the past. The rain cascading down its body made its skin look shiny, reflecting the light from Charles's auro. A large glow emitted from around it which matched its anchor. The hippo stared down the scarred man, ready to defend Charles.

The attacker laughed to himself and began to wave his blade about in a playfully circular motion, a demonstration of how easy he could wield his blade.

The spirit beast glanced at Charles and let out a soft rumble as if it were asking whether Charles was okay. Charles nodded back at the hippo which turned to face the attacker once again before letting out another deafening roar. The sheer power of the spirit beast sent a shockwave of energy that rippled in the ground and the air around them, causing the attacker to brace himself. The man simply smiled and nodded as if impressed by the power being displayed by Charles's spirit beast.

They ran at one another, the hippo bearing its large protruding teeth and the aggressor with his blade outstretched. The hippo smashed its head into him, sending him hurtling backwards through the field. He was quickly back to his feet, but the spirit beast was upon him with its large, gaping mouth wide open, attempting to bite him. The scarred man jumped back, narrowly evading the hippo's attack before regaining his balance.

The hippo attempted to bite again, only this time the man grabbed hold of the spirit beast's jaws, stopping it from biting down on him. Charles could not believe the strength this stranger was displaying; he should not have been able to hold ajar his spirit beast's jaws like that.

"You know how to wield that blade!" Charles called at the man. Suddenly fear gripped him when he realised what the stranger would be able to do to his spirit beast.

The man continued to struggle with the hippo, but finally pushed its head backwards, his hands slipping in the process due to the slickness of the rain. He managed to dive to the side, avoiding the enormous creature's powerful jaws once more as they came crushing down. The hippo quickly and instinctively swung its large, paddle-like tail out from the side, catching the scarred man in the ribs and sending him crashing to the ground again.

The scarred man got back to his feet, spitting some blood onto the floor. That twisted smile returned to his snarling face as he breathed heavily. The rain was bouncing around them as both stood their ground, the man staring into the eyes of the spirit beast that stood before him. Appearing unfazed by the hippo's power, the scarred man ran at the glowing spirit beast once more, blade outstretched, ready to continue the fight.

# CHAPTER 4

Arnold was flying again. At least, in his dream he was. The feeling of being so high up without a care in the world really was an inspiring, mesmerising place to be to gather your thoughts. He truly felt free here. He was not as high up as usual but again could feel the icy, tingling sensation of the wind against his brown and tan wings. It was truly sensational, like nothing he had experienced. Catching a gust of wind, he flew even higher, riding the wind to take in the view, and what a view it was, perfect for a painting.

The sky was bright blue and littered with the occasional white cloud. The wind was calm, making it easy to glide through the air with minimum effort. In the distance, snow-covered mountains looked like a cake that had been dusted with icing from above, the snow clean and untouched. At the lower part of the mountains, a picturesque sight of pine trees protruded from the ground, also slightly dusted with snow. At the base of the trees, the calming waters of a lake looked so bright and blue that if not for the mountains, it would have been impossible to differentiate it from the sky above.

Swooping down from the sky, Arnold came level with the lake, his feet touching the very cusp of the water with enough tenderness to leave a slight jet stream behind him. The icy chill of the water on his feet felt quite refreshing. Catching another gust of wind, he swept high up into the sky again so that he could see the vast fields and hills of the countryside. The buzz he experienced when gliding through the air was so exhilarating, Arnold had never experienced anything like this before and he didn't want this to end. Arnold gasped to himself, awestruck at the landscape that appeared to be never-ending. He wondered how far the land could actually go on for. When he reached the brow of another large hill, he was instantly drawn to something in his periphery that had become visible in the sweeping landscape: a building or a tower of some description sat at the top of one of the hills in the distance, too far to clearly make out any details. Intrigued, he set off towards the building to investigate further.

Arnold's heart raced as he was awoken by the loud, shrieking noise going off right next to his head. The noise was shrill and pierced his ears with such force, it caused a brief sting in his eyes.

Arnold couldn't help feeling annoyed with himself; it was Saturday, and he'd forgotten to turn the stupid alarm off. Arnold reached out in a daze, the oafish, tired motion knocking the clock off his bedside drawers. It went crashing to the floor, creating even more noise. He must have woken everybody up with that.

For a whole hour, Arnold tried in vain to return to his dream, but after tossing and turning without success, he decided he might as well get up. He sat up in bed stretched, letting out a large yawn before stepping into his slippers.

Downstairs, Arnold was greeted by a large banner in the front room which read in large, multi-coloured letters, 'HAPPY BIRTHDAY!'

"Happy birthday, sweetheart!" Eve came sweeping out of the kitchen and gave Arnold a suffocating hug.

Arnold's dad walked behind him and ruffled his already bed-worn hair. "Fifteen! How on earth has that snuck up on us, Eve?" he exclaimed. "Seems like only two minutes ago we were bringing you back from the hospital."

"Thanks Mum, Dad." Struggling to breath within his mum's grasp, Arnold shook his head and attempted to peel away her arms. He had been looking forward to his birthday, not for the gifts but for the fact that he was now at the prime age for his spirit beast to manifest, which was all he wanted. He knew it was only a matter of time, but could still not help feeling frustrated that nothing had physically happened to him yet. He felt that he would happily trade all his birthday presents just to know what his spirit beast would be, or to even just have a physical sign, a physical change. Was he stronger? Faster? More intelligent?

Arnold spent the morning making his way through a pile of birthday cards before starting to unwrap his presents. His favourite was the first-person RPG Xbox game that his mum and dad had bought him. No sooner had Arnold finished unwrapping his presents and got himself dressed, there was a familiar, rapid knock at the door. He opened it to find Otto standing there, his face lit up. The kind of face you would see with a three-year-old that had walked into a room filled with presents after Father Christmas had been.

"Well?" He paused. "Did you get it?" He was looking at Arnold with his eyes wide open like he'd had one too many cans of energy drinks and would burst if Arnold didn't put him out of his misery soon.

Arnold laughed. "Happy Birthday, Arnold, oh thanks, Otto, come in, Otto!" His sarcastic tone seemed to go over Otto's head, however, who simply looked at Arnold with a blank expression, oblivious to the sarcasm on display.

Otto was truly terrible at reading people and understanding

sarcasm was too much of an ask. He just didn't get it. "Well, did you?"

Arnold stepped to the side and smiled "I got it."

Otto beamed, and the two ran upstairs so they could test out the new game.

"I had another dream last night," Arnold told Otto a couple hours later as the boys played. "At the time, it felt so real but when I wake up, the more I try to remember it, the more distant it seems to become."

Arnold was sitting on his bed, while Otto was crossed-legged on the beanbag in the middle of his bedroom, engrossed in the new game.

"That reminds me," said Otto, "I spoke to my dad last night when I got home, and he told me to tell you –" he paused, concentrated on shooting someone in the game they were playing online.

"Get in, did you see that?" He looked over at Arnold, proud of the shot that he had just taken, eliminating the opposition in the game with a sublime headshot.

Arnold stared at Otto in disbelief at his ridiculously short attention span.

"What?"

Arnold let out a loud sigh. "Your dad told you to tell me *what*?"

"Sorry. He told me to tell you, well, apparently your dreams are most vivid when you first wake up. The longer you leave it after waking up, the less you will remember." Otto stuffed one of Arnold's birthday mint chocolate truffles into his mouth.

"Spit it out, Otto."

"Basically, you need to keep a pad next to your bed, and as soon as you wake up, you jot down the details," Otto said through a mouthful of chewing. "And better still, draw anything specific that you see." He smirked at Arnold, proud that for once he had contributed something productive to their conversation, like the cat that got the cream. This didn't happen with Otto often and Arnold knew he liked to savour these moments.

Arnold rummaged through one of his drawers until he found the pad he was looking for and placed this on his bedside drawers next to his alarm clock.

"I wonder if Everett had any dreams before her spirit beasts manifested?" He sat on his bed and sighed loudly, snagging one of the chocolates for himself.

"Think you should just ask her, mate."

Otto had a knack for stating the obvious.

"Maybe I will, when we see her later."

"You'll bottle it."

"Whatever."

Arnold felt a wave of jealousy come across him. It wasn't fair that Otto and all the others in his year at school were either showing signs of their spirit beast or able to summon one. But no, all he was left with was dreams of flying, and what use was that to anyone? Arnold didn't care what his spirit beast was, he just wanted something real to happen to him that wasn't a dream.

He picked up his controller thinking that maybe shooting some people might distract him for a short while. He slouched onto the beanbag that Otto had vacated in the middle of the room and set up another match for them to play. Otto picked up the other controller and the two began frantically bashing buttons. Arnold tried to push down his concern for time being, but he couldn't help but ponder the nagging question in the back of his mind: what if his spirit beast never showed up?

~

Some time later, Arnold heard the knock at the door he had been eagerly waiting for all morning. He ran down the stairs two at a time and flung the front door open to find his grandad waiting for him. Arnold adored his grandad and loved spending time with him. He would often call around after school to have tea with him. The two were incredibly close, and to Arnold, his grandad was the most important person in the world.

"Well, boy, are you going to let me in?" Elwood said. He had on a green jacket, dark cap, and striped blue and white scarf. He looked well for his age, with an athletic frame and eyes as dark as Arnold's.

"Happy birthday, Arnold." He opened his arms wide to welcome Arnold for a hug.

Arnold stepped forward into his grandad's embrace, the oaky smell of his aftershave clinging to his scarf.

"Thanks, Grandad!" he replied as he stepped back to make room for him to come in.

Stepping into the house, Elwood took off his hat and removed his coat. He always dressed smart and today was no exception; he had opted for a white shirt and a pale blue tie. He wore a green jumper over the top but the shirt and tie could still be seen due to the v neck style. He still had a full head of white hair which was slicked back, albeit slightly matted from wearing his cap. His eyes looked tired, yet still sparkled at the sight of his only grandson.

Arnold, Otto, and Elwood walked into the living room where Arnold's grandad passed him an envelope. Arnold opened this to find a birthday card with a picture of a monkey on it. Vigorously opening the card, Arnold was pleased to find twenty pounds had been put inside.

"Thanks, Grandad!" Arnold said sincerely.

Arnold's grandad sat down in his favourite chair. It creaked almost as loudly as he groaned, as though he had ran a marathon to get here even though he lived only a couple of streets away.

"I'm sorry it's only money this year, Arnold, but I really struggled with what to buy you this time." He leaned over and gestured for a cup of tea. Arnold left the room, returning a few minutes later with a fresh brew.

"You are growing up far too fast. Seems like only yesterday your mum and dad brought you home."

Arnold smiled to himself as his grandad repeated what his dad had said earlier that morning.

"Maybe you could get yourself some aftershave to impress the girls at school. I was courting when I was your age," his grandad teased.

Arnold felt a rush of blood to his cheeks and knew instantly that he was blushing, something that seemed to be happening more and more recently, which he hated. Arnold walked over to the fireplace and placed his card with the others that he had opened that morning.

"Do you think your spirit beast could be a monkey, like on that card, Arnold?" Otto chuckled.

Arnold shook his head. "Last I knew, monkeys didn't fly," he replied whilst rolling his eyes. He really was not in the mood to be wound up about his spirit beast, even if it was his birthday.

"What do you think his spirit beast could be, Mr. Ethon?" Otto looked at Arnold's grandad, an eager expression upon his face as if he hoped he could impart some much-needed wisdom on them.

Instead, Elwood tutted in disapproval of the conversation, which deflated Arnold further.

"Leave it, Otto," Arnold said, wishing he had not said anything. He knew his grandad didn't like talking about spirit beasts and kicked himself for letting Otto ask him about his. His grandad often became closed off at the mere mention of them.

"You want my advice?" Elwood started, his tone that of irritation. "Don't rush it, Arnold," he snapped. "Having a spirit beast is not all that it's cracked up to be. It's not all fun and games." Arnold's grandad took a sip of his tea and placed the cup back down on the table. "Wish the bloody things didn't exist. Don't get me started on those Spirit Wardens. If you just want to talk about spirit beasts then I will leave you boys to it and be on my way."

Arnold understood that he didn't like to discuss spirit beasts, but did he need to bite his head off like that?

Bernard and Eve walked into the room, so Arnold and Otto seized the opportunity to go back upstairs.

"What was that?" Otto looked at Arnold, gob-smacked at how blunt his grandad had been with him. "You okay, mate?"

Arnold attempted to brush it off like he was fine, but his grandad had really upset him. He knew he never liked to speak about spirit beasts or about his time as a Doyen, but it was devastating to be snapped at like that.

"Why is he so against them?" Otto pressed.

Arnold shrugged his shoulders limply, unable to explain as he did not know the answer. He had never spoken to his grandad about it due to the reaction he knew he would get, and whenever he approached his dad about it, Bernard simply told Arnold to leave it alone, so he did.

"Come on, we best head to town, otherwise we will end up missing the film," Arnold said, not-so-subtly attempting to switch the topic of conversation. Arnold was looking forward to taking his mind off his spirit beast for a while.

On the train, Otto offered his umpteenth theory about Arnold's grandad. "Maybe he has forgotten how to summon his spirit beast and that's why he gets grumpy when anyone talks about them? What *is* his spirit beast, anyway?"

"I don't know, Otto," Arnold sighed. "Neither my dad or my grandad have ever told me."

Arnold felt drained by Otto's persistence in coming up with a theory that fit. "Can we not just talk about something else?"

Arnold still felt deflated about how his grandad wouldn't speak to him about his spirit beast.

The two were so close about everything. Arnold spoke to his grandad about things he didn't even speak to his parents about, not even Otto. It really hurt him that he wouldn't even listen to him about his dreams or advise him about the changes that he would be going through soon.

Arnold couldn't dress it up. He felt let down by his grandad, but he picked himself up and forced a smile at Otto, determined not to let it spoil his birthday. After all, he was fifteen now, and before long he would have his very own spirit beast.

"Ahem, feet."

Arnold and Otto noticed the ticket conductor standing over them. The woman looked fed up, her eyes cutting through them both like daggers. They decided not to push their luck and quickly moved their feet off the seats. The boys looked a little bit sheepish but luckily for them, the train drew to a halt, and they knew they had arrived at the station.

When they reached the cinema, they found Everett waiting for them with her best friend George. Both girls had their spirit beasts summoned, messing around. Everett's boar and George's fox were chasing after each other, but overall the fox was more agile and too quick for the boar. The two animals were surrounded by a soft glow coming from the girls, purple for Everett and yellow for George. The fox jumped up on a wall near where Everett and George were talking. Everett's boar ran to the wall and let out a series of grunts, appearing frustrated at its inability to scale the wall like the fox had done.

"Watch this, guys," Everett said. For a moment, she concentrated heavily on her spirit beast, then switched her focus from the boar to the wall. The fox lay with its tail hanging down, teasing the boar. The boar jumped back and shuffled like it was readying itself for something. Then it threw itself at the wall, causing it to shake as the boar staggered backwards, dazed from the blow. The fox lost its balance and fell from its perch. Arnold, Everett, and Otto set about laughing, but George stood there stony faced, clearly unimpressed at what Everett made her spirit beast do.

George folded her arms and the three of them stopped laughing at once, bracing themselves for the lecture that they were about to receive.

"That is cruel, Everett! That could have really hurt your spirit beast! How could you be so irresponsible? If you misuse your spirit beast, there is a chance it will not summon for you. You have only just learnt how to summon it so don't ruin it by being reckless."

"Jeez, alright!" Everett replied, clearly wanting to move the conversation forward. George smiled back at Everett, probably knowing that this was the best she was going to get out of her. Everett and George had been best friends for as long as Arnold had known them, since even before George had started shortening her name from Georgina due to her complete dislike of the name that her parents had burdened her with.

George also had her own quirky fashion sense and did not like to conform to so-called social norms. Today she was wearing a long black-and-white-striped top that came down to just above her knees, three-quarter-length jeans, and her Doc Marten boots. As always, she was wearing her trademark beanie hat with just a tiny bit of red curly hair poking out from the front and back of it. George wasn't as abrupt or brash as Everett, but she was not afraid to speak up for what she thought was right or passionate about.

"You should start up your own campaign for spirit beast rights, George." Otto grinned as he tried to wind her up.

George placed her hands on her hips, clearly not appreciative of Otto poking fun at her. "Haven't you heard about the Aeigis Order?" she demanded.

Otto stared back at her blankly, looking as clueless as Arnold felt on the matter.

"What's the Aegis Order?" Arnold asked.

"Seriously, do you not try and figure things out for yourself instead of just accepting everything that the Spirit Wardens tell you? Luckily, I have my granny and her shop," George continued proudly. "She tells me everything she knows, there is so much more out there in the world."

George's granny was known as the town's only spirit sage, she had so much wisdom compared to others. Spirit sages were adept at potion-making and dedicated their lives to researching the bridge between this world and the spirit realm, where those gifted with the ability drew their links to their spirit beasts.

"That still doesn't tell me what the Aeigis Order is," Otto said.

"Think of them as an alternative to the Spirit Wardens. They have different principles that define them. Take artefacts, for example. The Spirit Wardens take these and hide them away, afraid that menials will use them to cause harm. The Aeigis Order would use those artefacts to research and help not just those with spirit beasts, but also menials connect to the spirit world."

"As much as I enjoy watching you educate Otto, come on guys! We need to head in otherwise we are going to miss the film." Arnold was trying his hardest to make sure the movie wasn't ruined by the other three winding each other up. "I'll pay for you, Everett, if you like. Otto will pay for George."

Otto looked at him disapprovingly. "Fine, I'll pay for George, it's a bit like a double date, this, isn't it?" Otto winked at George who shuddered at the mere mention.

Everett laughed. "Don't kid yourself, boys. I don't think you're George's type."

Arnold felt a rush of blood fill his cheeks once more and

instinctively spun away quickly to avoid the others noticing. What he would give to have just a fraction of Otto's confidence.

Otto turned and headed towards the entrance, always eager to get in first so that he could get his bucketful of popcorn and giant cola. The other three followed Otto and joined the large queue that had formed to gain entry to the cinema. After what felt like an age, they had finally gotten their tickets and snacks and made it down a dark corridor towards the double doors that were illuminated by a large number three. Arnold pushed one of the doors open with his foot before using his body to hold the door open for the others. He contemplated letting the door swing back at Otto, as this was something he would do, but this time he opted against this. As tempting as it was, he didn't want to come across as childish in front of Everett. Otto loved to play pranks on others, and it would have been sweet revenge to get him back.

They walked up the steps and shuffled along in the dark to find their seats. Arnold sat down next to Otto who placed his popcorn on his knee and scooped up a large handful, ready to shovel it into his mouth. Arnold, unable to resist the urge, surrendered to the compulsion and seized his opportunity; he nudged Otto's arm, knocking the popcorn in Otto's hand all over him and Everett. George let out a giggle of amusement.

"You got me," Otto whispered. "I'll give you that one, which now makes it ten-one to me."

"Shhhhh." There was an irate man behind them who did not appreciate them talking and laughing. The four of them sunk down into their seats and settled down to watch the movie.

As Arnold readied himself for the film, he placed his arm on the rest and realised Everett's arm was already resting there. He quickly pulled away awkwardly and noticed Everett give him a sweet smile. She moved her arm over slightly to allow him some space to rest his arm next to hers, and he nervously obliged. His heart raced and, bizarrely, he found his arm trembling as he placed it next to hers. His arm had never felt so heavy.

"Thanks," he whispered, and Everett returned a smile that reminded him just how pretty she was.

After the movie finished, Arnold, Otto, George, and Everett exited the building. Arnold squinted as his eyes adjusted to the natural light outside after being in a darkened room for the last two hours.

"Well, that's two hours of our life we will never get back," Everett said, evidently less than impressed with what she had just been made to endure.

Otto looked at her with pure disbelief. "What are you on about, Everett? That film was amazing." Otto was sci-fi mad, and even though Arnold also thought the movie was poor, there would be no convincing Otto as he tended to love and appreciate even the worst sci-fi films. Arnold thought back to when Otto made him watch a film called *Monster in the Closet*. It was awful, but the more cheesy and naff the film was, the more Otto enjoyed it.

"It wasn't that good," Arnold said.

Otto simply looked at Arnold with a smug grin before switching his gaze to Everett and laughing to himself. "Come on, we need to head back to the train station. Can't be late for your birthday tea, Arnold." Otto nudged Arnold to garner his attention and whispered, "Ask them if they want to come."

Nervously, Arnold said to the girls, "Are you joining us?"

Otto gave Arnold a smile like a proud parent.

"That's, if you want to – I mean, if you have things planned, don't worry . . ." Arnold could have kicked himself. Why was he now giving them reasons to say no?

Otto shook his head in disappointment.

"Erm, if that's okay?" Everett replied for the both of them, despite George looking less than impressed at her for accepting the invitation.

"That would be great!" Now Arnold felt pleased that Otto had encouraged him to ask, but even happier that Everett had accepted.

They walked back down the road towards the train station, still talking about the film with Otto arguing the reasons why it made such a good cinematic experience. On occasion, Arnold's eyes would meet Everett's, and he felt his heart race that little bit faster.

The weather suddenly turned, dampening the light atmosphere. It began to rain so heavily that they had to run the last hundred yards in order to get to the shelter of the train platform. The rain stung Arnold's skin as they were pelted with what felt like small stones. They raced under the shelter at the train station, the sound of the rain hitting the roof almost comforting to hear. Everett shuddered from the cold and huddled into George to keep herself warm. Otto shook his head like a dog shaking excess water from its fur, splashing Arnold who himself shook his arms to rid himself from excess rain.

"Where did that come from?" Otto finished shaking his head. The rain was bouncing off the floor and the noise from the rain hitting the shelter was incredibly loud. It sounded as if stones were being thrown at it rather than rain. Though the others cowered from the sudden storm, Arnold found it to be oddly therapeutic, almost hypnotic. He looked out across the field opposite them on the other side of the train station in a mesmerised state.

Right then, something caught his eye at the far corner of the field. Arnold focused his eyes and could see an old man carrying his shopping bag and another man in a long overcoat stood opposite him. They were staring at each other. The man in the long coat exuded hostility, his fists clenched.

"That's odd," Arnold murmured.

The others gave Arnold a puzzled look.

"What's odd, Arnold?" Everett asked, walking over to him.

Arnold pointed out to the field in front of them. "Over there, there's two men staring at each other." Arnold directed his friends' attention to the far corner of the field next to a footpath. The others followed Arnold's gaze, but their looks of bewilderment did not change.

Otto squinted. "I can't see anything." Everett and George shook their heads as well.

"Right there!" Arnold pointed again. He could see the two figures clear as day, and something about the interaction between the two men was giving him a bad feeling.

He was confused as to why it was so clear to him and not to the others. As Arnold focused more on the man with the overcoat, he saw him pull something from his jacket. Arnold recoiled, and a feeling of horror came over him as he realised that the man had pulled out a blade and was now running towards the elderly man. His intent was clear from his snarling face.

Without thinking, Arnold leapt down onto the track, climbed up the other side, and scaled the fence, dashing into the field.

Arnold was acting on instinct, but he had no idea what he thought he was going to do when he reached the other side. He just knew that the elderly man was in danger, and that he needed to help him.

Arnold stumbled and slipped through the mud as he ran, his feet becoming heavy as his trainers and jeans were soon filthy with the tar-like mud clinging to his legs. But he kept going.

Arnold felt as though his chest was going to explode, his heart was pounding that much. The rain was lashing against his face, the needle-like sensation stinging his skin. A bright flash lit up the darkened sky in front of him, followed by an almighty roar like he had never heard before. His ears began to echo from the noise, and he knew instantly that a powerful spirit beast had just been summoned.

Over his shoulder, Arnold could hear the muffled sound of the others calling after him, and in no time, Otto had caught up with Arnold.

"Over there!" Arnold panted. "Do you see it now?"

Otto nodded as he kept pace with Arnold, a steely look in his eye.

The elderly man was slumped on the floor, while the man in the overcoat engaged in combat with a large, battle-worn hippo. Arnold was close enough now to see the hippo's cracked skin, which appeared gouged out by claws and teeth from previous quarrels, its skin rubbery as the rain cascaded over its body. The spirit beast stood its ground with its mouth open, baring its large, razor-sharp teeth.

His attacker appeared unfazed by the spirit beast's display of power, however, and simply ran at the hippo, jumping into the air and over the top of it before plunging his blade into the beast's back. The hippo let out an almighty roar and slumped to the floor as the man walked over to its side, drawing his blade from the spirit beast's back.

"How is that possible?" Arnold called to Otto as they continued their run to help. It was a well-known fact that no ordinary weapon should be able to interact with a spirit beast. "That must be an artefact!"

The elderly man let out a cry that seemed to mimic that of the spirit beast he was intrinsically linked to. If their connection had been bound together by a rope, it was now frayed to almost bare.

The hippo let out a low grumble as it began to absorb back into the body of the elderly man, its power spent. The attacker walked towards the elderly man with a crooked smile on his face, breathing heavily as though he had enjoyed every second of their conflict.

"Give me your power," the man demanded angrily. He stretched out his arm towards the elderly man, grasping his blade tightly within his hand and pointing it directly towards him. Arnold was too stunned to act as he watched a glow of light move from the elderly man towards his assailant. It moved like a fog, drifting slowly across the ground as the injured man groaned in agonised pain.

The stranger was absorbing this man's spirit beast, but how?

Arnold was suddenly distracted by the soft, yellow glow of the fox and the purple glow of the boar as they ran past him, making easy ground on the difficult terrain. The two spirit beasts ran straight at the attacker, the fox leaping through the air and into the back of the man. The boar followed this up by charging into the back of his legs, forcing him to lose his balance. The man lost his footing and fell into his muddy surroundings as Otto and Arnold started shouting to draw his attention away from their friends.

"Over here!" Arnold said, waving his hands frantically.

"Why don't you pick on someone a bit younger, you coward!" Otto yelled, picking a stone up and launching it towards the man.

Their distraction worked. The man's face contorted with rage as he clambered to grab hold of his blade from which the dark green fog of the hippo's power was drifting back towards the unconscious old man like a cloud of dust in reverse.

"Fools," he growled, "you have no idea what you are doing." He climbed to his feet and strode straight towards Arnold and Otto.

"Now what?" Arnold muttered under his breath to Otto, still trying to regulate his breathing after the sprint across the field.

Otto glanced back at Arnold. "Run!"

The pair set off running again, knowing that they had the

full attention of the attacker. The next thing Arnold knew, the darkness behind them was illuminated by a bright orange glow followed by a powerful blast of energy that engulfed them as if they were in the midst of a storm.

A radiating glow lit up the area around them as though it were daylight, pulsating with energy raw from the spirit world. There was a sudden density to the air, an unnatural feel around them. Something didn't feel right. It was nauseating, and Arnold's heart thundered so hard against his ribs that he thought it may burst from his chest.

A deafening roar shook him to the core, one that was closer than Arnold would have cared for, and he felt something strike him from behind, the considerable force knocking him to the floor. Winded, Arnold tried to pick himself up from the ground, his arms shaking as adrenaline coursed through his body. He looked over to his side to see that Otto had also been knocked off his feet, except he looked unconscious. Arnold rolled onto his back and desperately searched around for what must have been the attacker's spirit beast, but he could not see it. All he could see was the face of the man stood in front of him.

The stranger had thick, long dark hair that was untamed, and his eyes were dark and wide with rage. The rain continued to wash over him and pattered against the long, flowing black jacket that hung over his hulking frame. His hands were clenched tightly around a blade that looked more like a tusk than a knife. An orange glow emanated from the blade, wrapping his hand and arm in a spectral hue that cast light against his face like a flame. The scars that engulfed his face left large, cracked indentations within his skin, from above his right eye all the way down to his lip, showing his horrific disfiguration.

The man gave Arnold a wicked snarl. "What were you hoping to achieve? Did you actually think you could stop me?" He stepped towards Arnold with murderous intent in his eyes.

Arnold had never known fear like it. This man was going to

kill him. Bile rose to the back of his throat as Arnold choked on his breath, all the while scurrying backwards to draw some distance between him and the scarred man. His heart racing faster than ever, he felt stressed enough to vomit, and his head spun with anxiety that tore through his body.

"You attacked me from behind like a coward!" the man growled, anger emitting from every pore of his body. "I'd like to see you try again, now that I am facing you! You dare to stop me, and now you clamber away from me like the coward that you are. You will face the consequences of your petulance." His voice was hoarse and gravelly.

He lashed down and struck Arnold across the face, then pulled him up slightly before raining down another heavy blow against his head.

In a flash, Arnold saw white light and stars as dizziness took over. He had never been struck before, he never wanted to again. His head instantly throbbed, his vision blurring. He felt as though his brain had rattled from the blow. As he gathered himself, he could feel his cheek burning from the first blow and the warm sensation of blood coming down his face.

"You think that your spirit beasts would be able to stop me and save him." The man spoke through gritted teeth so tight that it was a feat on its own that they did not shatter. He leaned forward and grabbed Arnold by the scruff of his neck, picking him up from the floor as if he were filled with air. "You think you are saving a poor, defenceless man, but you know nothing. You have no idea what he did to me!"

Arnold tried in vain to avoid eye contact as the scarred man's own eyes burned into his face as he was hoisted into the air. He flailed his arms and legs as he tried to escape the man's grasp, but it was to no avail. He was at the stranger's mercy.

Pulling back his blade, the attacker readied himself to finish Arnold off, but caught him glancing over his shoulder. A defiant smile forced its way across Arnold's trembling lips.

"Something distracting you?" the man sneered, incensed by Arnold's cockiness.

"There is one thing," Arnold started, "those spirit beasts weren't ours." Arnold nodded towards the elderly man.

The scarred man looked back over his shoulder to see Everett and George tending to the injured man. They were crouched by his side, the glow of their spirit beasts shrouding around them.

Arnold swung his leg back and aimed a kick at the scarred man with as much strength as he could muster, making contact with his stomach. The man let out a roar of rage and threw Arnold through the air, bouncing him off the ground for several yards, wrapping him in a coat of mud. Arnold came to an abrupt stop as he rolled into a tree, his arms shaking as he attempted to pick himself up from the ground once more. He struggled to his feet, waiting for the next blow, but it didn't happen. Instead, Otto had thrown himself on the back of the attacker and begun to frantically hold on as if trying to choke him. Otto was stronger than Arnold, but he was still only a boy and the assailant grabbed hold of him and spun, tossing him into the ground with a thud. Otto's body skipped across the ground until he clattered into Arnold's feet, tripping over him and collapsing in a heap on his friend.

Sirens rang out as lights flashed across the field – the Doyens had arrived.

Their attacker looked at the old man who was still being tended to by Everett and George, then turned his attentions to the approaching sirens. He glared at Arnold and Otto. "This is not over!"

Arnold gathered himself and anticipated another blow, dragging himself to his feet once more, but when he raised his head, the attacker was gone, the sirens growing louder and louder. Arnold hobbled over to check on Otto, who was groaning and gasping for breath through winded lungs.

"What happened?" Otto sat himself up, holding the back of his head.

"Your shoulder!" Arnold panicked when he noticed that Otto's t-shirt was torn and bloody. Arnold felt a wave of nausea, but managed to gather himself as he tended to his friend. Otto grimaced as he put his hand over his shoulder, then looked to see his hand covered in blood. "Ow!"

Arnold knelt to support him. "Are you okay?" he said. "I think we just saved that old man's life."

George began pointing and shouting, directing the Doyens to where they were.

As Arnold's dad and another Doyen set off running across the field towards them, Otto looked up at Arnold and groaned. "Your dad is going to kill us."

# CHAPTER 5

"And you are sure that's everything that you can remember, Arnold?" Bernard was stood next to him in the hospital bay, waiting for the doctor to come and give him the once-over. Arnold's face throbbed and his head felt like it had been split in two, but aside from that, he felt okay, unlike Otto who had ended the night having a clawed strike down his shoulder blade.

"I've told you everything, Dad." Arnold had lost count of how many times he'd gone over what had happened. He knew he had to but with his head feeling like it was, he was becoming a little frustrated at having to repeat himself. "Is the old man okay?" Arnold asked. "Do you know who he is?"

His dad shuffled around nervously, seeming to have more than one thing on his mind. Bernard was the highest-ranking Doyen in the area, meaning that everyone would be looking at him for answers over the attack. He wouldn't just have his seniors to respond to, but the local media, too.

"The old man is called Charles, and he is not in a good way," he started. "As it stands, he is in a coma and is not responding." Bernard sat in the chair next to Arnold's bed and let out a large, weary sigh. "Are you absolutely certain that you saw Charles's spirit beast beaten by a man who had no spirit beast summoned? Are you certain that it looked like the attacker was absorbing his spirit beast?" Bernard looked deep in thought, clearly disturbed by the night's events. His eyes were slightly bloodshot, and dark, purple bags were forming under his eyes.

"I know what I saw, Dad. The man was fighting with the spirit beast and when he beat it, he began to draw it from the old man. He was using the blade." Arnold just wanted to rest. He was so tired, his eyelids felt like they were weighed down by stones, and he fought desperately to keep his eyes open.

Apparently sensing that his son was struggling, Bernard ran the tap beside them and filled a glass of water before passing it to Arnold. "Here you go, son. Remember, the doctor said you shouldn't sleep, not until your results are back."

"Thanks, Dad," Arnold took the cold water and took a large gulp, savouring the cold sensation as it trickled down his throat.

"So, he had an artefact, a vessel to transfer the old man's spirit beast to use as his own," Bernard continued. "If this is true, then we must inform the council immediately. The Spirit Wardens have most artefacts in their protection for this very reason. Menials cannot be trusted with the power that these artefacts can grant." Bernard spoke quickly, as if his thoughts were spilling out of his mouth as fast as they were entering his head.

"What's to say he was a menial? I think Otto's shoulder shows he summoned a spirit beast."

"Only a menial would use an artefact like that. Why else would he attack and try to steal a retired Doyen's spirit beast?"

"I think he knew him," Arnold said. He fought back a wave of nausea as another hot flash came over him. "The way he spoke, how angry he was, I am sure he spoke about revenge."

"You have no idea how lucky you are, Arnold. How you

managed to not get yourself killed is beyond me, especially if he was able to fight a spirit beast on his own. That itself shows how powerful he must be. It is simply unheard of."

"I just wanted to help, Dad. I couldn't leave an old man there being attacked." Arnold finished off his cup of water.

"I'm proud of you, son, honestly, I am. You have shown incredible bravery when others may have run. This could've gone so wrong, though." Bernard shuddered, as if imagining losing his son. "I don't know what, you know, if you'd –"

Arnold smiled. "I understand, Dad."

The ruffled blue curtains that surrounded Arnold's bay scraped back, startling Arnold as the metal hoops grated against the rail that fixed the curtains to the ceiling.

"Master Ethon, my name is Doctor Shira. I am here to give you a once-over, if that's okay. Is it okay if I call you Arnold?" Her voice was soft and reassuring.

"Sure."

Doctor Shira pulled out a small torch from her dark blue scrub top and shined this in Arnold's eyes to check for signs of concussion. Bernard's phone rang and he gestured to Arnold that he needed to take the call, leaving the bay to answer as if the blue curtain was a barrier to any sound inside and outside of the cubicle.

Doctor Shira raised a finger. "Okay, Arnold, can you follow my hand?" She began to slowly move her hand from one side to the other.

Arnold focused on her finger, following the instructions he had been given.

"You have a mild concussion. Nothing a few days' rest won't solve. I will let your parents know that you will need a few days off school to recover."

"Sorry, Doctor Shira, did you say parents?" Arnold knew instantly what was coming, and an avalanche of looming dread suffocated Arnold in an instant.

"Where is he, is he here!" Arnold easily recognised his mum's voice as she hurriedly burst into the bay, her face pale and gaunt with worry.

"Goodness, look at you!" Her eyes were filled with tears, her cheeks blotted from where she had been crying.

Grabbing hold of Arnold, she squeezed him that tightly that he thought his head was about to pop. She pulled away from him and moved his head to one side to give him a quick check-over herself, revealing the cut on his head that had been stitched.

"What were you thinking?"

Bernard walked back into the bay. "Eve, give the boy some breathing space, you're going to suffocate him."

"Bernard, how could you let this happen?" she scolded. "It's your job to keep the town safe, did you not pick up on this man's energy?"

"Now isn't the time, Eve," Bernard said calmly.

She sat down in the chair next to Arnold and squeezed his hand tightly, rubbing her thumb against its back.

"Mr. and Mrs. Ethon, Arnold will be fine to go soon, we just want to finish these observations and I will prescribe him some painkillers. He needs to rest. You should both be very proud of him. He saved someone's life," Dr. Shira said with a reassuring smile.

"We are, worried sick but proud. Thanks, doctor." Eve smiled wearily.

"I will be back shortly with the painkillers, then Arnold is free to be discharged and go home with you both."

Dr. Shira exited the bay, leaving Arnold and his mum and dad in the cubicle.

"I have just been to check on Otto," Bernard said. "He is fine, but he had to have stitches on the slash he received on his shoulder. It must have been the attacker's spirit beast that did this, as it is a claw mark. He is luckier than you are if he was attacked by a spirit beast." Bernard placed his hand on Arnold's shoulder. "Mr. Whittaker is here. He wants to speak to you."

"Mr. Whittaker?" Arnold said, puzzled. He knew that Mr. Whittaker was his dad's boss but didn't understand why he would come and visit him at the hospital.

At this moment, Arnold could hear a well-spoken male voice from behind the curtain. "I'm looking for an Arnold Ethon."

Bernard left the cubicle and returned with Mr. Whittaker and a woman that Arnold was unfamiliar with. Mr. Whittaker was taller than Bernard and slender in size. He dressed very smartly with his purple shirt standing out from his dark pinstriped suit. His slicked-back blond hair made him look more like a banker than an Elder for the Spirit Wardens.

The woman beside him, who gave off a somewhat nervous disposition, was dressed like a librarian with her red-and-white floral blouse tucked neatly into her skirt, her blond hair bobbed to her shoulders. She looked to be in her mid-twenties, quite young to be working with the Spirit Wardens.

"Arnold, this is Mr. Whittaker and Miss Rushton," Bernard introduced them. "Mr. Whittaker is my senior at the Spirit Wardens, and Miss Rushton is the regional secretary for us."

"Please, call me Raine." Her softly spoken voice reassured Arnold, his nerves beginning to set in now that his dad's boss was here to see him. "Mr. Whittaker has something he wishes to discuss with you," she continued. "How are you feeling?"

"I'm okay," Arnold replied. "Cracking headache, though." He raised his hand up to his head.

Raine placed her hand reassuringly on Arnold's arm and cast him a warm smile. Arnold knew straight away that he liked her. She seemed nice, genuine, and warm.

Mr. Whittaker let out a subtle cough to capture Raine's attention who withdrew her hand straight away and stepped back from Arnold, allowing her boss to step forward and stand next to Arnold's bed.

"The old man that you saved is called Charles Grey," Mr. Whittaker informed him. "He used to be a Doyen, a very powerful one at that. Not only did you and your friends save his life, but you also stopped his spirit beast from being stolen. What's worrying is that this attacker, who is most likely a menial, is in possession of an artefact that we are unaware of. This is why the Spirit Wardens like to keep hold of artefacts, to stop them falling into the wrong hands. Rest assured, our resources are now extended to finding this madman and acquiring this blade he is in possession of." Mr. Whittaker's well-spoken voice matched the expensive-looking suit that he was wearing.

"But I think he had a spirit beast, how could he be a menial?" Arnold asked, thinking of Otto's injury.

"Because of the artefact he had in his possession. Did you see what he summoned?"

Arnold shook his head. "No, sir. All I remember was the darkness lighting up behind me with an orange glow and the roar from whatever chased us."

"I see. Well, if you do remember any more details, make sure you tell us. We might be able to figure out what the artefact was."

"All I know is that the blade of his dagger looked like it was made from a tusk or something."

"Raine, please notify the other Doyens in the area to be looking into this at the Athenaeum. The sooner we catch this man, the better." Mr. Whittaker commanded an air of authority about him, his nose slightly raised in the air.

"Yes, sir," Raine said timidly. "I will get to it right away." And she left.

Mr. Whittaker continued, "Now, there is something else that

I wish to discuss with you, Ethon." Mr. Whittaker's body language changed as if suddenly he was uninterested.

Arnold braced himself to be reprimanded in some way. He found himself tense as he waited for what he knew was coming. He'd been waiting for the lecture all night, knowing that he'd put himself and his friends in danger.

"We, I mean the Spirit Wardens, would like to extend an invitation for you to join us at the Athenaeum."

"I'm sorry, what?" Surely he'd misheard Mr. Whittaker. "You're asking me to join the Spirit Wardens?" Arnold's heart began to race. This was what he had wanted his whole life, but he must have been dreaming. He had taken a heavy blow to the head, after all. "But I am only fifteen?"

"Not just you, your friends that all assisted have been invited, too," Mr. Whittaker was quick to correct Arnold. "Although the two girls – was it Miss Harris and Miss Vulpine? – have already declined."

"But how exactly are we allowed to join the Spirit Wardens?" Arnold asked, unable to process what he was being told.

"A loophole," Bernard said, the colour quickly draining from his face. "Are you sure we should do this, Mr. Whittaker? He – my son is still some way off from adulthood."

"He is just a boy, he is too young for all of this," Eve protested, her face a picture of worry.

"I do not agree with this," said Mr. Whittaker. "However, the Spirit Wardens have instructed me to extend an invitation to him. There is an expectation that you accept. For some reason they are very interested in you, but I do not know why." Mr. Whittaker moved his hands to behind his back before continuing. "In saving the life of Charles Grey, a Doyen, you have earned the right for this invitation. It does not mean that you will be successful given that the expectations are extremely high, and from what I understand, you do not yet have a spirit beast. This is most unheard of, to be in the Spirit Wardens without a spirit beast. I advise at this stage to not let it be known amongst the wider community. This cannot be common knowledge," he said disapprovingly. "It could potentially cause chaos not just in Lancashire but outside the boundaries, too."

"Is this true, Bernard?" Eve asked. "Is what Mr. Whittaker is saying true?"

Bernard nodded. "I am afraid so, Eve."

"What about his dreams?" Eve blurted out, much to the disapproving look of Arnold's dad.

Mr. Whittaker clearly heard what she said, but seemed to choose not to acknowledge this, his attention fixed on Arnold.

It was quite clear that Mr. Whittaker was not fully on board with the Spirit Warden's invitation, but Arnold did not care. He had just received an invitation to join the Spirit Wardens and despite his horrific headache, this was the best day of his life.

"Should you accept, I expect you to arrive at the Spirit Wardens next Monday following the end of your school day. That should give you sufficient time to recover." Mr. Whittaker turned to leave the cubicle. "Bernard, I will see you in the morning for debriefing," he added as he left.

Arnold beamed at his dad, who did not appear to be as happy as he was at the news. "What's up, Dad?" he asked.

"I'm happy for you because I know what this means to you," Bernard replied, "however, I know what you will have to go through in order to join, and I do feel you're too young for this. It's your decision, Arnold. If you join, at least we can train you how to defend yourself. In case this man comes back."

A wave of worry came over Arnold and suddenly his heart felt heavy. "Do you think he will come after us?" Arnold asked.

"It's the only reason I would want you to join," Bernard responded. "If you start to receive some training, you may be able to harness your spirit beast and defend yourself if he was to show up again."

Eve cast Arnold's dad a thunderous stare. There was something more to this whole situation, something that they were not sharing with Arnold.

"I don't have a spirit beast though, how can I join the Spirit Wardens if I could still be a menial?" Arnold's mind raced with all the ways he might fail as a Spirit Warden.

"You are forgetting one important fact, Arnold – your spirit beast *has* started to manifest."

Arnold stared blankly. He had no idea what his dad was talking about.

"You said you could see right across the field as clear as anything when everyone else couldn't. You could see everything that was happening from a lot farther than you should have been able to."

The blank expression on Arnold's face began to waver as he slowly began to understand where his dad was going with this.

"You have enhanced vision, Arnold. That's quite a rare power to develop."

In all the commotion of the day, Arnold had completely forgotten about this. In an instant, he felt as though a huge weight had been lifted off him. Finally, he had something to go off. Now all he needed to do was research what spirit beasts could be linked to enhanced vision. His mood lifted to a new height, the excitement of his spirit beast starting to manifest causing him to grin like the Cheshire Cat.

"You need to rest, son. You have had an eventful birthday, one you'll likely never forget," Bernard continued, a weary look on his face. "The doctors are happy for you to come home with us. Have a think-over the next couple of days about Mr. Whittaker's offer."

"But Mr. Whittaker made it sound like I didn't have a choice."

"You always have a choice, Arnold," Eve said, moving to

help him stand from the bed. It was quite clear that she was against him joining the Spirit Wardens at the Athenaeum.

"I'm okay, Mum. I can get up by myself," Arnold told her.

As the three of them made the journey home, an uncomfortable silence filled the car as Arnold realised that his life was about to change forever.

ARNOLD SPENT the next day in his bed sleeping, suffering from the worst headache he had ever experienced thanks to the concussion. His mum kept creeping into his room to check on him from time to time and ensure that he was drinking enough water. She tried her hardest to get him to eat some food, but he did not have the appetite for eating.

Arnold was awoken by raised, muffled voices coming from downstairs. He checked his alarm clock by the side of his bed to see that it was just after midnight. He felt confused, wondering who would be at his house this late. In a daze, he crawled out of bed and walked across his bedroom, stopping momentarily when a head rush kicked in after his sudden movement. Once he had gathered himself, he crept across the landing to the top of the stairs in an attempt to see who was in the house. As Arnold came around from his concussed sleep, the two voices became clearer. They belonged to his dad and his grandad. He began to listen to the conversation closely, confused as to why the two would be having heated words.

"Bernard, I am telling you that Arnold is too young to go. He may have shown he has enhanced vision but that is not enough, not for the level of training that he will be exposed to. It's too soon. What if –"

He cut himself off and lowered his voice, looking around the room as if making sure they were alone. Elwood's tone was assertive and hostile towards Arnold's dad, something Arnold had never seen or heard before. "What if his spirit beast is a –"

The floor creaked where Arnold stood, stopping his grandad mid-sentence. Arnold could have kicked himself. It was strange hearing his grandad talk about spirit beasts, but Arnold was pretty certain his grandad was just about to say what his spirit beast could be.

"You know what I mean, Bernard," he spoke again in an even quieter voice. "The Spirit Wardens will take him away if they were to find out."

"Dad, it's not entirely my decision. He needs to learn to defend himself and to harness his spirit beast. We can't be fully sure what it is yet, we are just guessing. Besides, the Spirit Wardens seem pretty insistent that he joins."

"Do you think they know? Do you think they know what his spirit beast could be? You haven't told anyone about his dreams, have you?" Elwood pressed.

"Of course not. I haven't spoken to anyone at the Athenaeum about Arnold or his dreams. I am not a fool," Bernard said dismissively. "They don't know what Arnold's spirit beast could be, let alone that."

"What if it is, though?" Elwood said, shaking his head from his seat. "He has been having dreams of flying. Just like your mum used to."

Arnold was confused now. Were they were talking about his grandma? She was someone very rarely spoken about, having died before he was born.

"I know that, Dad, but it's too risky to discuss, especially if anyone realised what his abilities could be." There was a tremble in Bernard's voice that brought fresh worry to Arnold. What had his parents not told him when he was in the hospital? He could tell there was something his mum and dad were hiding from him, and now he knew his grandad was in on it, too.

“Have you gone into detail with him yet about his dreams and what they could mean?” his grandad quizzed.

“Not yet. The timing hasn’t been right. He has been asking questions, but I need to know for sure that his dreams and powers are linked.”

“He needs to know, Bernard. Not only would it be hard to master, but there is a large chance that he could be corrupted. You don’t need me to go into detail around that again. Need I remind you of your mum, what it did to her?” There was a crack of pain in Elwood’s voice that Arnold did not like, his voice croaking and wavering as he spoke about Arnold’s grandma.

Arnold wondered what they meant by corruption, a term he was unfamiliar with when it came to spirit beasts.

He didn’t know anything about his grandma, so his curiosity was heightened. He leaned closer to the stairs, wanting to carry on listening to what was being said, desperately trying to absorb as much of the conversation as he could.

“You don’t need to remind me, Dad. I lived through that with you.” Bernard’s voice began to raise, an air of frustration in his response. “I grew up without her because of it. Arnold is a good boy. Whatever his spirit beast is, he will still be a good boy and for that reason alone, he shouldn’t be told yet. Not until he is ready. I don’t want it to influence him.”

Arnold felt intrigued by his dad’s comments. What was so bad that they couldn’t just tell him what they thought his spirit beast was, and what had happened to his grandma?

“I don’t want people to judge him,” Bernard continued, taking an assertive stance with Arnold’s grandad. “We will have to see how he develops. If there are any signs, I will get him to leave the Spirit Wardens. Before anyone realises.”

“Do you not think that is too much of a risk? What if someone realises before you have a chance to pull him out? You say you want to prepare him, but how can he be prepared if he does not know about what happened all those years ago? It's part of our family's history. What if he is going through what your grandma did? I won't have it, Bernard, and if you won't tell him, then I will."

Bernard exhaled, seeming exhausted with the conversation. "Then you need to give him some space while I try and figure this out. He is my son, and I will protect him how I see fit." He slammed his hand down on the coffee table for emphasis.

Arnold's grandad looked saddened by Bernard's comments, clearly hurt by the ultimatum that had just been placed on him. "He's too young for the initiation, Bernard. Please think about this, he is just a boy." Fighting back tears, Elwood continued, "he is my grandson, my only grandchild. The Bloodbound Ritual, it's traumatic, it might change him."

"I can't go against the will of the Spirit Wardens. He has been invited. If he doesn't go now, then I don't think they will offer it again when he is older. The council does not take kindly to being rejected."

Arnold felt an uneasy wave of pressure which only served to add to his nausea. If he said no now, would that mean he would not have another chance?

"That isn't a bad thing, Bernard."

"How can you say that? You were an Elder before you retired."

"I have my reasons. I have respected your decision to join the Spirit Wardens. That doesn't mean I agree with you and Arnold joining."

"Well, try being honest with me, I know there is something you are not telling me," Bernard said, his expression turning furious. "He isn't being told about Mum, and he certainly isn't being told about his spirit beast. We will deal with that when he finds out what it is naturally. All we will do is worry him if we tell him now. I'm not going to change my mind." Bernard paused for a moment, the clock ticking in the corner the only noise ruffling the uncomfortable silence. "I think you should leave." There was a curt shortness to Bernard's words, an exasperated coldness in his voice.

Arnold's grandad looked crestfallen. His shoulders dropped and he bowed his head before turning and walking to the front door. He left without another word being spoken. Arnold felt a buildup of anger inside him that was overpowering. He had never felt anything like it before. He contemplated challenging his dad but decided against this, seeing that he was already keeping secrets from him.

Arnold crept back to his bedroom, trying as hard as he could not to make any noise and draw attention to himself. "How dare he," Arnold muttered to himself while pacing in his bedroom, still unsure what to make of all of this.

After ranting to himself for the best part of an hour, Arnold got in bed, his mind still whirling with questions and his head spinning from his concussion. What spirit beast were they referring to? What had happened to his grandma? Why was his grandad worried about the Spirit Wardens, when he had been an Elder in their ranks?

Arnold intended to find out.

# CHAPTER 6

Arnold remained in his bed for the next two days as he continued his recovery from his concussion, in part because he did not want to leave his room and see his dad. Bernard had thrown himself into work, and Arnold knew it was because of his disagreement with Arnold's grandad.

Arnold was frustrated at the secrets being kept from him and didn't feel he was ready to talk to his dad yet, even though he had questions he wanted answering. His plan was to see his grandad, but since the attack, his mum had kept him under strict observation, meaning he wasn't able to sneak out of the house.

Arnold was sat on his bed reading, finally able to now that his concussion was pretty much gone. The book in question was *Spirit Beasts: Unlocking Your Potential*, a self-help guide from his favourite spirit beast expert, Davies Gregor. Arnold had most of his books and envied that he got to travel the world exploring the histories behind different cultures and their ancient links to spirit beasts. On the cover, the guru was sat on a cliff edge looking out over a ravine, his owl spirit beast summoned next to him.

Arnold was busy scribbling notes on ways that he could

trigger his spirit beast manifestation when his bedroom door creeped open and his mum poked her head in.

"Otto is here to see you," she said, stepping back to let him into the room. "I thought a visit might cheer you up."

"Thanks, Mum,"

"How's the head?" Otto asked, peeking his head inside the door frame. His face showed a combination of apprehension and excitement.

"Better," Arnold said, waving Otto in, "how's the shoulder?" He put his writing pad back on his bedside table.

"Not as painful now. As soon as I was back from the hospital, my mum and dad put one of their traditional remedies on it. My dad reckons it's a claw mark from some form of big cat, although he's not sure which one. Maybe a tiger." Turning around, Otto lifted his t-shirt to reveal the four gashes on his shoulder. The stiches were visible through the thick, dark green mixture of herbs that his parents had rubbed into the wound. He lowered his t-shirt with a goofy look on his face. "Pretty cool, eh?"

"I wouldn't say cool." Arnold shook his head. "Looks pretty sore that, so your dad thinks it could be a tiger?"

"Only a specialist would really know and there were none available at the hospital because let's face it, this kind of spirit beast attack never happens," Otto said, throwing himself onto Arnold's beanbag. He winced at his over-eagerness and brought his hand up to rub his shoulder.

"Maybe my dad or someone at the Athenaeum could help? Did my dad speak to you and your parents about the offer from Mr. Whittaker?"

Otto shrugged. "Yeah."

"Everett and George have said they don't want to accept the invite, I can't believe they wouldn't take up the offer. This is such a great opportunity." Arnold's voice became elevated at the mere mention of the Spirit Wardens.

"Not everyone is as keen on the Spirit Wardens as you, Arnold." Otto smirked. "I said yeah though. Couldn't let you do it on your own, could I?" Otto picked up Arnold's game controller and switched it on, his focus turning to the TV screen as he continued to talk. "Think about it, Everett and George have their spirit beasts whereas we don't. They are both more advanced than both of us put together. It's only because of tradition that we have been invited. We challenged someone who was stronger than us to save the old man despite the danger. Speaking of the old man, how is he?" Otto asked Arnold.

"My mum said he is still in a coma and he is not showing any signs of waking up. His spirit beast was stabbed so that must have really hurt."

Otto, now immersed in the game, shook the pad as if it were going to help him. "My dad reckons that there is something we're not being told by the Doyens. Keeps asking me about what we saw because normal weapons cannot interact with spirit beasts. Only certain artefacts can."

"That's another question that my dad needs to answer then." Arnold swivelled out of his bed and placed his feet on the floor.

"Do you know what else is interesting?" Otto paused the game and pulled out a copy of *The Oswaldtwistle Advertiser* from his rucksack, then tossed it to Arnold. "There has not been a single story on the news or in the local paper about what happened."

"Doesn't surprise me, my dad is good at keeping secrets at the minute." There was a bitterness to Arnold's voice, causing Otto to raise his eyebrows.

Arnold spent the next twenty minutes filling Otto in on the conversation he had overheard between his dad and grandad.

"The plot thickens," Otto said. "Do you actually think that your dad will stop you from seeing your grandad?" He slouched into the beanbag, managing to keep his focus on Arnold without getting distracted by the Xbox.

"He can try," Arnold said defiantly.

"So you think they know what your spirit beast is?"

"I think if I speak to my grandad, he will tell me everything. I have so many questions that need answering and I think I'm more likely to get them from my grandad than my dad." Arnold was already planning in his head that he would go and visit his grandad one day after school this week. He'd had to take a few days off following the events from his birthday. To be honest, Arnold felt glad that he hadn't gone into school for the last few days. He would have struggled to concentrate from his concussion, but he also could not stop thinking about what his grandad had said. He felt that both his grandad and dad knew what his spirit beast was and that it could be linked to a spirit beast that hadn't been around for a long time. Arnold also wondered about his grandma. Just who was she, and what had her spirit beast been?

There was another knock at the front door followed by the sound of footsteps rushing up the stairs. Everett and George came bundling into the room and rushed towards Arnold and Otto, wrapping their arms around them as if they had not seen either of them for years.

"Ow," Otto scolded Everett who had inadvertently caught his shoulder, causing him to turn slightly paler.

"Sorry, we just wanted to see you guys, we were told to leave you for a few days and we just wanted to make sure you were both okay." Everett then switched over to Arnold and gave him an equally restrictive hug.

Arnold savoured every second of the embrace. He had never been hugged by a girl before, and sweet, candy-like fragrance hung off Everett. Her grip was tight, and Arnold was surprised by how strong she was.

Otto proceeded to fill Everett and George in on everything

that they had just been discussing and answered the same questions that he himself had asked a short time ago.

"This is so messed up," George said. "I mean, who does that to an old man? To see his poor spirit beast stabbed like that was awful. I had no idea that you can be so in tune with your spirit beast that you feel the pain that it feels. Do you think it might work the other way around where the spirit beast feels the pain of their anchor?" She had a determined look on her face.

"What about the scarred man?" Everett wanted to throw her two pence in.

Arnold shrugged, unable to give any further information. "Apparently the Doyens are searching for him, but they have no idea who he is or what his motive is. He has just vanished into thin air."

"People don't just vanish," George replied. "I think there is something we're not being told."

Arnold had a horrible feeling deep down about the scarred man. "No one will know until the old man wakes up," he said. But what if his dad was right, and there was a chance that the attacker would come after them for interfering? After all, they had stopped him from stealing the old man's powerful hippo.

"That's why we need to go join the Spirit Wardens," Otto added.

Everett glanced from Otto to Arnold. "I take it you guys have accepted the invitation then?"

"They asked us too, but it's just not for us," said George, seating herself on the floor in a cross-legged position. "Besides, I am too busy helping out at my granny's shop." Arnold knew that George was more interested in learning to be a traditional healer like her granny. "It is a great opportunity for you two, you should go for it."

"We need to be prepared for if the scarred man comes back," Arnold told them. It was the one thing that he did agree with his dad on.

"My parents have said I can join," Otto said excitedly. "My dad was not so keen though. Keeps harping on about family tradition. I am used to that from him, though."

George looked down at her watch. "I'd love to stay longer but I need to head to my granny's shop, I'm meant to be helping her this afternoon. Everett, are you coming?"

Everett nodded.

Otto got to his feet as well. "I'll head back with you two, see you at school tomorrow, Arnold."

The three of them left Arnold's bedroom, leaving Arnold alone to stew in his whirling questions. Now he just had to wait for his dad to get home.

~

An hour later, Arnold was sat with his mum at the dinner table making his way through the lasagna that she had made them all for their tea.

He leaned forward to pick up a piece of garlic bread from the centre of the table. "Dad's home late again." He knew he needed to speak with his dad but couldn't help but get a dig in against him.

Eve let out a sigh, disheartened by the way that Arnold was being with his dad. "You two need to sort this out, you're both just as stubborn as each other. He should not have spoken to your grandad like he did, but he just wants to protect you. He really thinks it's best you go to the Spirit Wardens with him."

Arnold took a frustrated bite out of his garlic bread. "I have decided I will go, but I have questions I need answering."

"Make sure you talk to your dad then, when he gets home." Eve seemed sheepish, as if this were a conversation she would rather avoid.

The front door opened, and Arnold's dad entered the house.

"Nice of you to join us," Arnold said glumly, unable to help himself. He may have needed to speak with his dad but he was still mad at him.

"Arnold!" Eve scolded him. "Do not speak to your dad like that." Arnold didn't get told off often, and he knew he may have just overstepped the mark.

The next fifteen minutes felt incredibly uncomfortable as everyone finished the lasagna and garlic bread without speaking a word. After they finished, Arnold cleared the table and went through to the kitchen to clean the dishes.

"Need a hand, son?" Bernard's voice came from behind him as Arnold stood with his hands in the washing up bowl. Bernard picked up the folded tea towel that was neatly placed over the handle of the oven and began drying the dishes as Arnold washed them.

Arnold fixed his gaze on the bowl, choosing not to engage. He needed answers but he didn't quite know how to broach the subject because of the frustration he was feeling.

His dad continued, despite Arnold's reluctance to talk to him. "I am just trying to protect you, Arnold. You're not ready to know everything yet. You're too young. I was eighteen before your grandad told me everything." His face looked pained, and Arnold did not know how to respond. "There is a certain type of spirit beast that you are showing signs of through your dreams. I have not wanted to tell you this, as I don't want it to impact you for the wrong reasons, I want you to be able to connect to your spirit beast naturally. Well, to a certain extent. If you accept the offer, your Bloodbound Ritual will boost your connection like no other way. If I told you what I thought your spirit beast was, it could delay or change how it manifests, by changing the way you respond to things." Bernard seated himself on a barstool and put his head in his hands. "I didn't mean to speak to your grandad like I did, and I feel terrible for it. We both want what is best for you, but we just have different ways to help and support you."

"What happened to Grandma? And is it linked to whatever spirit beast you think I may have?" Arnold had asked the questions before he had time to think.

"It's not my place to tell you what happened to your grandma, but yes, I do think your spirit beast may be linked. It is too much of a coincidence for my liking. If you want to know what happened to your grandma, you need to speak with Grandad. I don't think you're ready, but I will respect your choice. However, your grandad has gone away for a week or so to clear his head. When he gets back, Arnold, I promise you, you can speak with him, if that's what you want."

Arnold believed his dad but was now intrigued as to where his grandad had gone. Bernard walked across the kitchen and placed a hand on Arnold's shoulder, which Arnold found comforting.

"Starting tomorrow, you and Otto need to come to the Athenaeum with me every day after school. Only there can you be taught how to truly master your spirit beast, whatever it may be. This will not be easy for either of you. The training is gruelling and you two are very young to begin this. It is unheard of for children your age to be invited into our ranks, but we have to honour tradition." Arnold's dad sounded apprehensive with his words as if he wasn't fully sure that they should be joining him at the Spirit Wardens, despite his previous assertions that Arnold needing training to protect himself. "Then there is the Bloodbound Ritual," he added.

"You have mentioned that a few times. What is it?"

"Your initiation. It's a ceremony that all invited to train in the Spirit Wardens have to go through. That is all I can tell you."

"What will happen?"

"Arnold, I can't tell you. It could alter the ritual."

Arnold left it there and went to bed that night feeling a combination of excitement and nervousness about what he was going to experience tomorrow with Otto. For the first time, he was actually going to go inside the Athenaeum. This was amazing to Arnold, who had dreamed about this for so long, not realising that his training would be starting earlier than he ever could have anticipated.

Arnold lay on his bed, his mind whirling with thoughts of the scarred man, Charles Grey, his grandad and grandma, and joining the Spirit Wardens. He still had so many questions and a part of him felt that he may not get all the answers he wanted, but at least for now, he was getting somewhere.

Eventually, he drifted off to sleep.

~

ARNOLD WAS FLYING AGAIN. But this time, something felt different, *he* felt different. He felt bigger, more powerful. His wings were larger than usual and he seemed to be covering ground a lot faster than before. His large, black wings propelled him through the air with ease. It was sensational. Looking below at the fast-moving ground beneath him, Arnold could see his large shadow, but he was unable to make out his shape. It was clear that this was not the same animal that he normally dreamt about, but he found that he liked this shape more.

Across the vast fields in front of him, a building that felt familiar towered from atop a large hill. Arnold headed in the direction of the building, covering ground at an incredible pace, much faster than what he was used to. The feeling was exhilarating, and the adrenaline that was pumping through his body made him feel as though nothing could stop him.

As he reached the building, he adapted the position of his wings to start bringing himself to a halt before gliding down to get closer. Now at a slow glide, he could see clearly the stone tower in front of him, surrounded by broken, rickety fences that looked as though a strong gust of wind could blow them over. The tower appeared old and untidy, with the dark grey stones covered in green moss that was creeping up from the ground, covering three-quarters of the structure. Its windows were sealed from the inside with big, rusted metal panels preventing anyone from looking in. A large chimney protruded from the triangular roof that looked as though it was ready to collapse in on itself, and another copper-coloured sheet covered a small window just below the chimney.

Feeling drawn to the small window, Arnold began to glide towards it, but suddenly he was overcome with the sensation of falling. Out of nowhere, he felt completely unable to fly. To his shock, Arnold began to hurtle to the ground at speed, the rocks below fast approaching. He tucked his head low into his chest and wrapped his wings around himself, bracing himself for the impact.

Arnold woke up startled and fell from his bed. His sheets were ruffled as though he had been flailing around like a koi carp that had jumped out of a pond. Arnold and his sheets were drenched with sweat, and he sat bolt upright, instinctively grabbing his pen and pad from his bedside drawers where his alarm clock sat. He began to sketch the tower that he had just seen in his dream in as much detail as he could muster. Arnold was not the most talented artist, but he did the best he could. When he finished, he sat staring at the tower he had drawn. He couldn't help but feel that this tower had something to do with his spirit beast, and furthermore, he was certain that if he could find this tower, it would help him manifest it. He felt drawn to it like a magnet. That tower had the answers he was looking for, he knew it.

And now he had to find it.

# CHAPTER 7

As soon as it was the morning, Arnold headed straight downstairs with his pad to show his dad what he had seen. Bernard was already sat at the table making his way through his jam on toast.

He looked at the picture for a short while before closing the pad and sliding it back towards Arnold across the table. "Sorry, son, I don't recognise it."

Dejected, Arnold left his pad on the table and went back upstairs to shower and get ready for school. His mood lifted, however, when he remembered that today was the most special of days. Today was the day he was going to join the Spirit Wardens.

"Make sure you pack your gym clothes for after school," his mum's voice echoed up the stairs.

Arnold couldn't wait to finally learn more about spirit beasts. All he had to do was make it through another day at school. After grabbing a shower and getting changed, Arnold came back downstairs and had some breakfast. While finishing off his cornflakes, his dad walked back into the room.

"I'm heading off to the Athenaeum now," Bernard told them, giving Eve a kiss as he made his way to the front door.

Eve picked up Arnold's pad and placed it in a drawer in the hallway, not saying a word.

Arnold quickly ran upstairs to grab his backpack and gym clothes before sprinting down the stairs.

Eve stopped him and gave him a kiss on the head. "See you tonight. I hope everything goes well for you at the Athenaeum tonight. Trust your dad." Although her words were supportive, her tense body language said the opposite, and Arnold knew his mum did not want him to join. He gave her a reassuring smile, then walked straight out of the front door. At the bottom of the path, Otto stood waiting for their normal walk to school.

"Today's the day!" Otto called. "I can't wait for school to finish, is it half three yet?" He put his hands in his pockets and set off walking next to Arnold. The two of them headed towards school to get the most boring part of the day done with. The weather was matching Arnold's mood: bright and sunny. Today was going to be a good day.

"I had another dream last night. This was different though, like I was something else. I felt more powerful than before, I felt like I was bigger, it was so strange. I saw this haunting tower, made from large stone walls which sat at the top of a hillside."

"You think it's a real building? Did you manage to draw it?"

Arnold nodded, answering both of Otto's questions in one movement.

"I'm hoping it is real, maybe it links to my spirit beast." There was a hopefulness in Arnold's tone, he wanted it to be real so badly.

They made it to school with Arnold filling in Otto with the rest of the details.

"So, it definitely felt different?"

"Yeah, this was not the same animal I normally dream of. It felt incredibly powerful, like nothing I have ever felt before. I felt angry, a real rage inside me that I could not get out of my system."

"Wait up!" The voice called out from behind them, and Arnold instantly recognised it as belonging to George, her distinctly broad northern accent making her stand out from most others. She had her beanie firmly planted on her head with the same bit of red hair poking down the front of her forehead.

"Ask her what she thinks," Otto prompted.

"About what?" George asked, catching up to them.

"Arnold's latest dream, says he was flying again. Did we tell you?"

"Tell me what?"

Otto laughed to himself. "Clearly not. Arnold has super sight."

Not appreciating the title that Otto had taken it upon himself to give to his newfound ability, Arnold quickly corrected him. "It's more enhanced vision."

"That's different. Wonder what that could mean. What about an owl?" George suggested.

Otto burst into laughter. "Maybe you *are* a bat."

George simply rolled her eyes. "Bats use sonar, you moron." She turned to Arnold. "Ignore him, Arnold. There are lots of other spirit beasts this could be linked to."

"Like what?"

"Erm, well, maybe this is what we need to look into for you. Your auro is developing and you're now showing signs. You know what comes next. I'll ask my granny after school, you should maybe swing by the shop sometime."

Arnold was holding little hope in this but was just glad that he had shown some form of sign. All he had to do now was figure out what his spirit beast was going to be. Arnold couldn't help but feel that this enhanced vision was a bit of a useless attribute, though, and felt jealous that he had this lame power when Otto had become more athletic.

"When did you get yours?"

"My fox?"

"No, your squirrel," Otto teased.

George shook her head before answering Arnold's question. "About six months ago, I guess. I noticed I had become better at gymnastics and about a month after that, she appeared to me when I was in the garden at home practicing. It was amazing."

"How long after you turned fifteen did it appear?"

"Erm, about two months after my birthday."

"Sweet, mine must be due at any time then," Otto exclaimed.

The bell rang for registration and the three of them said their goodbyes and split up to go into their separate classrooms. Arnold sighed to himself as he sat down. At least he would be able to start looking into this more when he started training with the Spirit Wardens tonight. More than ever, he wanted to know what his spirit beast was going to be.

The rest of the school day seemed to drag as all Arnold could think of was getting to the Athenaeum and the initiation. He just tried to get on with it, keep his head down, and complete his work. Even the threatening glares of Kaden and his cronies couldn't bring Arnold's spirits down today.

Finally, when he had made it to the end of the day, Arnold stood by the entrance to the school just past the main gates, waiting to meet up with Otto. He began pacing, his nerves kicking in with the anticipation of joining the Spirit Wardens. Arnold looked at his watch for the tenth time, wondering where Otto was, who was late as usual.

"You will be fine!" Everett's voice rang out from behind him. He turned to find her walking towards him, laughing. "You're making me nervous with all that pacing. You need to try and calm yourself down." Everett scrunched her hair back into a ponytail and fastened it into place with the bobble she had around her wrist.

"Are you sure you don't want to join us at the Athenaeum?" Arnold wanted to make sure that the two of them were absolutely certain about their decision.

"Honestly, it's not for me, and George is more interested in following in her granny's footsteps. Besides, I want to head to university when we finish college. I have no interest in being a Spirit Warden."

George caught up with Everett and said, "Good luck, Arnold, I am sure you will be great." She gave Arnold a warm hug, and Everett followed suit and did the same. Arnold savoured the moment, the sweet smell of Everett's hair and her perfume infatuating him further. Maybe, just maybe, when Arnold had become a member of the Spirit Wardens, he would have the confidence to ask Everett out.

"Let us know how you get on," George said before the two of them set off down the street, walking arm in arm.

"Ready to go?" Otto called out as he exited the maths block and greeted Arnold at the gates.

"Seriously? I have been here fifteen minutes and you are asking me if I'm ready?" Arnold could be dumbfounded at times around how ignorant his friend could be.

"Needed the loo, nerves and all that." Otto caught up with Arnold and the two of them set off in the direction of the Athenaeum, neither knowing what to expect when they got there.

Before long, the two of them were stood in front of the large building, staring up at the big stone steps to an entrance that Arnold had wanted to walk into since as long as he could remember. Now that the opportunity had finally presented itself to him, his legs felt like they were made of lead, unable to take the initial steps he needed to move forward. Taking a deep beath, he raised his foot and took the initial step as though he was about to climb a mountain, a combination of nervousness and excitement circling around Arnold's mind.

When they reached the top, a large, circular oak door loomed in front of them, inscribed with words from an ancient language that Arnold did not understand. The wording covered the outside edge of the door, leading to a large symbol in the centre. Upon closer inspection, the symbol carved out on the door appeared to be a representation of the local Spirit Wardens. In the centre was the large rose that represented Lancashire, and sitting just below as if climbing over the petals themselves was an intricate bee. The carvings on the door were like nothing Arnold had ever seen before and he stood for a while admiring the workmanship that had gone into it. Suddenly the door opened from the inside, pulling backwards and then rolling to the side in such a smooth motion that it hardly made a sound. This was expert workmanship at its finest.

Arnold's dad appeared in the doorway, a proud yet nervous smile greeting them both. "Don't just stand there, come in," he told them, beckoning them forward.

Otto stepped forward first with Arnold following closely behind, his chest pounding. He was feeling even more nervous now, and as he walked into the building, he had no idea what to expect next.

Inside, he was taken aback at what he saw, almost feeling disappointed. They were standing in what appeared to be nothing but a normal-looking lobby. Just beyond the door were a few seats and then opposite them a reception area. The black-and-white marble floor which resembled a chessboard was freshly polished, causing the light to reflect from the expensive-looking, intricate chandelier above.

"It's – it's modern," Arnold exclaimed in surprise.

His dad burst into laughter. "What were you expecting? Chairs made of stone? We have to update the building to keep it fresh. Don't worry, though, we have all the traditional chambers at various points around the Athenaeum. You will see soon enough." He guided Arnold and Otto past the reception area. "Raine, you met Arnold at the hospital. This is his best friend, Otto."

The receptionist stopped what she was doing and gave them both a warm smile. "Welcome to the Athenaeum."

"She's fit," Otto muttered under his breath, his eyes almost popping out of his head.

Arnold laughed and nudged Otto as the two of them grinned at each other.

She was sat behind the desk, her blond hair straightened which stopped at her shoulders. Her eyes were fixed on her computer screen as she typed away on the keyboard without looking at it. A fine skill in itself.

The two of them gave an awkward wave and Raine glanced up to offer a smile before returning to her work. Arnold's dad led them beyond the reception area and down the hallway before stopping and opening a door. "Come on in, this is my office." He gestured for them to enter and followed them inside. "Please take a seat."

The room was tidy and as office-like as you could imagine. A large, dark wood desk was positioned on the far side of the room, with a pile of old leather-bound books, parchment, a note pad, and pen sitting neatly on its surface.

Arnold couldn't help but feel that this was very businesslike as they sat down in the two chairs that sat opposite his dad's desk.

"Right, I just wanted to go through what will be happening this evening," Bernard said, taking a seat at his desk. "The first thing I am going to need you to do is get changed out of your uniforms. I will show you where the changing rooms are shortly. There will be two tunics in there for you. Put these on in preparation for your Bloodbound Ritual. Now, normally this intensifies the connection between you and your spirit beast. However, you two do not know their forms yet, so this process will aid you in discovering this. I don't fully know what will happen, as normally you already have your spirit beast when we carry this out. Should be interesting."

"Bloodbound Ritual? Already?" Arnold had read that there were different initiation ceremonies specific to each Spirit Warden rank, but none of the books published had any details about what the initiation entailed. It was a secret saved only for those who joined. His nerves intensified as suddenly everything seemed even more real.

They left their backpacks in the office and Bernard led them farther down the corridor, guiding them to the changing room. The room looked similar to a gym's changing room, with lockers and pegs to hang clothes off. To the side was an ornate sink carved from granite, and towels folded neatly into piles sat on a table beside the sink.

"Your tunics are hanging up over there. I will be waiting outside to take you up to the chamber where your initiation will take place."

Bernard left the room, leaving them to get ready. At the far end of the changing room, two dark green tunics were hanging up just like Arnold's dad had told them.

"This has got a bit weird," Otto pressed.

"Everyone that's accepted into the Spirit Wardens has to do this," Arnold said, though he privately agreed with Otto's assessment.

"Well, it's not like you can die from it," Otto said, but then his face fell. "You don't think we could die from it, do you?"

It was a thought that hadn't occurred to Arnold, and he could have kicked Otto for planting the unnecessary seed of fear in his mind. He began to get undressed before picking up the tunic to examine it in more detail. The dark green material was stitched together with fine, gold thread, and the front of the tunic boasted the same rose and bee that were on the front door, embroidered into the fabric.

The two of them placed their tunics on and headed back out to the corridor where Bernard was waiting for them. To Arnold's surprise, his dad had gotten changed into a dark blue tunic which had the same symbol as theirs on it, but his had more intricate embroidery, including four stripes on his right sleeve.

Bernard noticed Arnold staring at his sleeve. "It's my rank," he explained shortly. "This way."

Arnold and Otto followed Bernard down the hall before stopping at a lift door this time. Pressing the button to call the lift, Bernard then stood silent, his hands crossed in front of him. The lift doors opened and the three of them entered.

Arnold shuffled in next to his dad, wondering what was about to happen to them. "Where are we going?" he asked, his voice wavering as his nerves began to show in his voice.

"We are going to the chamber at the bottom of the Athenaeum. That is where the Bloodbound Ritual will take place." Bernard entered a code into a keypad on the wall of the lift and the doors shut. The lift shuddered before beginning its descent. "If at any time you don't want to continue, just let us know and we will stop. What you are about to experience will hurt but it is all part of the process, and it will not put your life in danger. I need you to trust me on that."

"What's Bloodbound Ritual mean?" Otto quizzed, taking the advice they were just given in stride.

"You will know soon enough."

"That's all you're going to say? Come on," Otto pressed for more information.

Letting out a sigh, Bernard looked forward at the doors of the elevator. "It is a bloodletting."

As Arnold and Otto looked at each other blankly, Arnold could feel the colour drain from his face.

"I'm sorry, what?" Arnold asked.

But a moment later, the elevator doors opened.

Bernard just gave him a look, clearly indicating he would say no more. "Follow me," he said.

They followed Bernard out into the chamber which was dimly lit by flames around the room. His ceremonial robes draped across the floor in a smooth transition making it appear as though he was gliding across the ground like a spirit.

Arnold couldn't make out much of the darkened room, but he could see stone pillars lining up either side of the chamber, each with what looked like their own intricate patterns inscribed. He stared intently to bring them into focus, realising the shapes looked like faces cast into the stone. The lighting in the room was too dark to make out any specific details. Beyond the pillars, all Arnold could see was darkness. His attention was then drawn to the centre of the chamber where a man stood behind a stone casket. Shadows concealed his face, but Arnold could see that he was wearing the same tunic that his dad was. The man had his tunic open from his chest with symbols and markings that Arnold did not recognise.

The man's gaze was firmly fixed upon them, interested in no other in the chamber but them.

"Step forward." His deep, well-spoken voice echoed through the chamber, sending a chill down Arnold's spine. The nature of the voice did nothing to settle Arnold's nerves, which were getting steadily worse. At this point, his legs felt as though they were made of iron, rusted and slow moving, the tremble in him making it hard to walk at all.

Arnold was hesitant, only shuffling forward at a slow pace, in part due to the heavy feeling but also because he could not clearly make out the floor in front of him. He and Otto steadily moved towards the Elder who remained stood behind the stone casket, their footsteps echoing throughout the chamber.

"Redburn, Ethon, you are brought here to take part in the

ancient Bloodbound Ritual. You saved the life of a retired member of the Spirit Wardens and thus have been invited to complete the ceremony that has been passed down for nearly a millennium. Completing this ritual will enable you both to start on your journey of truly mastering your auros, a path that will enlighten you, a voyage you will be guided through by your spirit beasts. Only once you have completed this voyage will you be able to call yourself Doyens." His words were well-rehearsed, inspiring Arnold who had his eyes fixed on the shadow-laden face before him, accepting the darkness that surrounded him.

"Are you ready to proceed?"

"Yes," Otto replied, assured in his response.

Arnold felt unsure whether he could go through with this, his nerves still not settling. He wished he could be as calm and cool as Otto was.

The masked man paused, turning his attention to Arnold. "Are you ready to proceed?" he repeated.

"Yes," he said with a gulp.

"Then we shall begin," the Elder replied, his voice sounding even deeper than it did before because he was projecting his voice. "You have been approved entry to this Spirit Wardens because of the bravery you have shown in combat against someone incredibly stronger than you." He paused for a short while before continuing. "Without consideration for your own safety, you both stepped into the path of danger to protect another, and this is the path that Doyens follow." He stepped back from the stone casket and rubbed a substance across his face. "It is because of this act that you have been approved to enter this ancient Athenaeum, undertake the Bloodbound Ritual, and join the ranks of the Spirit Wardens." Placing his hands in the air, he began to motion in a circular fashion whilst humming loudly. His hands glowed a light green colour, slightly illuminating the area around him. "Doyens are finely in tune with their auros, enabling them to combine their energy with that from their spirit beasts. Spirit beasts are not only there to guide and protect us when we are in need, but they are also there to protect others. We are connected to our spirit beasts with the very lifeforce that runs through us all. Capture, not kill. That is the way of the Spirit Wardens, and that is what you must always remember." The man began to chant whilst continuing to move his hands in a circular motion.

Arnold could not understand the language that was being spoken, but he found the motion of the glowing hands soothing, as though he was falling into a hypnotic trance. Arnold was mesmerised and in awe of what he was witnessing, trying to take everything in.

The Elder abruptly stopped chanting. "The lifeforce that I speak of is your auro, the conduit between your auro and your spirit beast is your blood."

Arnold was intrigued as to what the man was alluding to.

"In order to truly connect your auro to your spirit beast, we must shed your blood to enable the transition from their world to ours. This is the ancient tradition of the Spirit Wardens passed down from the Elders." There was a calmness to his voice that Arnold did not expect given what was being asked of them.

Shed blood, what on earth? Arnold's stomach sank. He hadn't realised that when his dad had mentioned bloodletting, he'd meant it literally.

"That's where the bloodletting comes in then," Otto whispered, mirroring Arnold's thoughts.

Arnold could no longer see the man stood before him. Instead, he had morphed into what looked like glowing fireflies circling around each other in a smooth motion, as though they were dancing around each other.

How could Otto be so calm about this?

"As part of your initiation you will be required to let your blood spill into the casket before you. This casket is the grave of an ancient Elder who once protected this land, his bones consecrated before you. In completing this, you will encourage your spirit beasts to connect with your auro, making you more in tune with them." The man knelt before the casket, his hands still glowing. He leaned forward and picked something up, and when he stood back up, his outstretched arms revealed the soft, green glow of a blade in his hands.

Arnold's heart plummeted. What on earth was the man going to do to them with the blade? Arnold felt strained and conflicted. He trusted his dad, but he did not know this man, or trust him. His heart sank, beating faster than ever before, adrenaline pumping through his body now. Beginning to panic, Arnold looked around the room for his dad, seeking reassurance that everything was going to be okay, but he couldn't see him anywhere in the darkness that engulfed the rest of the room. Otto appeared to be completely unfazed about what was happening around them and what was being asked of them. Arnold finally noticed his dad stood by one of the pillars, illuminated slightly by the flickering flames nearby but mostly hidden within the shadows. He seemed calm and collected, observing everything that was happening, and this brought a little calm for Arnold's nerves.

Remembering his dad had told him to trust him, Arnold tried his best to steady his nerves, reminding himself that he and Otto were a lot younger than the usual age for doing this initiation.

"Hold out your left arm, Redburn. Ethon, you hold out your right," the man commanded.

Without hesitation, Otto stretched out his left arm as requested over the top of the stone casket. Arnold wished he could be more like Otto who was coming across as completely calm and collected, whereas Arnold felt like a quivering wreck. He put his right arm forward over the casket, his hand trembling. The more he focused on trying to stop his hand from shaking, the worse it got.

"Roll back your sleeves."

Arnold and Otto were both complied, rolling their sleeves to the top of their arms. "Now, make the connection even stronger by holding hands."

Walking around from behind the casket, the man manoeuvred himself to Otto's side. He then drew the blade level with the top of Otto's arm and began to project his voice again. "With this blade, I will offer your blood to the spirit gods to enable you to become one with your auro." With this, he pushed the blade against Otto's flesh.

Arnold instantly felt queasy, shifting his gaze to straight ahead of him, just about keeping control of his jellified legs.

Otto grimaced but overall seemed to be in control of the pain he must have been feeling, though he clenched his fist into a tight ball. He looked focused and determined as the man lowered Otto's arm to a forty-five-degree angle, and the blood started to flow down his arm, dripping from his clenched fist into the stone casket.

The man then moved to Arnold and pressed the blade against the top of his arm. "With this blade, I will offer your blood to the spirit gods to enable you to become one with your auro."

Arnold's heart was now racing at a pace he had never experienced. He could hear each heartbeat as if a drum were beating loudly in his ears. He winced as he felt a searing pain in his right arm, gritting his teeth as he tried not to make a noise. Just as with Otto, the man lowered Arnold's arm, which became crimson as his blood began to make its way down his skin and drip into the casket. Unable to hold it in any longer, Arnold cursed the air as he tried to deal with the intense pain. His head began to feel fuzzy and his legs grew even weaker.

"Focus, Arnold," Bernard's voice came from beside him as

he materialised from the darkness. He was carrying a flaming torch that burned with an unnatural, light green colour.

Walking straight towards the casket, Bernard lowered the torch into the blood-filled stone grave. The entire casket lit up into green flames and Arnold gasped, thinking it would burn him. But Arnold could not feel the heat against his skin as he would have expected, despite how close he was standing to it. If anything, the sensation was soothing, and a sense of courage overcame him. Suddenly he felt like he could take on the world, his fears slipping away as the flames danced in front of him.

The green fire began to rise into the air above them, dancing around as though putting on a show for Arnold and Otto. The flames split into two sections which began to swirl around one another, motioning in the same circular pattern that the hooded man had been gesturing with his illuminated hands. The man and Bernard began to chant again in tandem, and to Arnold's shock, the two separate flames began to take shape. In front of Otto, the fire formed the shape of a paw with sharp claws. Arnold shifted his focus to the dancing flame that was in front of him, which began to flicker. Arnold waited in anticipation, eager to find out what form the flame would take. Was he about to get a major hint as to what spirit beast he had within him?

The flame flickered again, which was strange as Otto's had not done this. Otto's had formed its shape in a smooth, seamless motion. Arnold looked towards his dad questioningly, but Bernard appeared equally as perplexed as he was. The flame quivered and morphed into the form of a wing, spiked and covered in what looked like scales. But almost instantly, it flickered again, this time changing shape into a wing covered in feathers. The flame then began sputtering back and forth between the scaled wing to feathered in quick succession.

The Elder's eyes widened as he watched, and Arnold instantly knew that something wasn't right.

"This can't be!" Bernard blurted out.

The flames let out a blast that knocked the Elder and Bernard backwards, away from the two boys. The unnatural inferno seemed to move of its own accord as green fire traced the path of blood from the casket up Arnold's and Otto's arms, until it reached the cuts made by the blade. Strangely, Arnold could not feel the heat from the flame crawling up his arm. The sensation was comforting, and the throbbing sensation in his arm began to subside. After a few seconds, the flames extinguished themselves. Arnold inspected his wound to find that it had healed, leaving only a thin scar where the cut had just been.

"The Bloodbound Ritual is complete," the Elder declared. "Your connection to your spirit beast has been maximised. Bernard, may I have a word?"

Bernard stepped out from the shadows.

"Did you see?" the Elder demanded, as if Arnold and Otto weren't still standing there.

"Yes," he replied, "does this mean what I think it does?"

"It does." The Elder turned to Arnold, who waited with baited anticipation. "It appears that you have a split auro, Arnold. Your spirit beast has yet to decide its true form. This is incredibly rare." The Elder had a concerned expression on his face, and he seemed to direct his next comment at Bernard. "Did you see the forms that the flames took?"

"I did," Bernard replied, looking pale.

"If that form is what I think it may be, I must inform the Spirit Wardens."

"I understand, sir."

Arnold felt like the two of them were talking in riddles and wished they would just tell him directly what was happening.

Bernard turned and faced the boys. "How are you both feeling? You both did incredibly well there." Arnold could tell that his dad was attempting to divert their attention. He could not believe how nonchalant he suddenly appeared.

Otto had a look of wonderment all over his face "That was amazing!" he exclaimed "You okay, Arnold?"

Arnold stood in shock at what they had just witnessed. He couldn't understand why his arm felt normal, despite being cut with the dagger just moments before. Even more bizarrely, he could not remember feeling any pain during the ritual, it was as if his memory of the pain had been completely wiped. "What animals did the flame show?" he asked, desperate to understand what he had just witnessed.

"You are on the path to finding this out," the Elder told him. "We can't tell you. You must discover this for yourselves." The man gestured for the two of them to roll down their sleeves. "Now, you must research the hieroglyphs that appeared in your Bloodbound Ritual. This was an indicator of the spirit beast each of you have. You will have access to the literature in the Athenaeum to aid you with this task."

"Why didn't the flames burn?" Otto quizzed.

"Because they were not born of this world."

"You mean they are from the –"

"The spirit world, yes."

"Boys, follow me back to the changing rooms," said Bernard. "Once you have dressed, I will take you to the Athenaeum." As Bernard began to walk towards the lift, Arnold and Otto quickly followed. The doors opened instantly and the three of them entered. "Was that Mr. Whittaker?" Arnold asked.

"It was, Arnold. Remember, he is the Elder, so he runs this Spirit Wardens here, as well as all the others in the Northwest. It is his job to conduct all the Bloodbound Rituals in Lancashire." He pressed the button on the lift, selecting the ground floor. "Only an Elder can facilitate the Bloodbound

Ritual. Only they have been shown how to access raw energy from the spirit world."

The lift doors opened, and Bernard escorted them back to the changing rooms.

"Get dressed, then come see me at my office."

Arnold's and Otto's bags had been delivered from Bernard's office. Arnold removed his tunic and examined his new scar in the large mirror. The scar covered the width of his arm, running smoothly from one side to the other. His arm still felt mostly numb but had begun to feel a bit fuzzy as though he were being gently jabbed with dozens of tiny needles. Arnold was dumbfounded that his arm had already healed and that he was no longer feeling any pain or in any form of discomfort.

Otto checked out his own scar. "That's pretty cool," he said appreciatively. "This will make us 'edgy' at school, you know. What type of spirit beast do you think yours is? I am one hundred percent certain that mine is a big cat, I hope it's a tiger. I can't wait to tell my dad that I am keeping in with family tradition. He will be well chuffed."

Arnold began to get himself dressed whilst replying, "I think it's safe to say that mine is something that can fly, given the wing that the flame turned into. But there are so many birds out there, it would be impossible to guess what it would be." Arnold pulled his t-shirt over his head. "I need to know more about what a split auro means for me."

Otto laughed. "Trust you to not have a simple auro. No wonder you don't have any signs apart from your super sight."

Arnold was a little taken aback by Otto's comments and the insensitive nature of them. "Glad you find it funny," he replied sharply. "We can't all have it easy like you, Otto."

"No need to snap."

Arnold left the changing room without saying another word to Otto. He knew he shouldn't have been feeling like this. He should have been on top of the world after finally seeing inside a Spirit Wardens and completing his initiation ritual, but in truth, he felt deflated at what he perceived to be another setback. “Why for once could it not be straightforward for me?” he muttered to himself. “Why is it me that has to have a split auro?”

Nothing positive seemed to be happening to him when it came to his spirit beast. He had a split auro which didn’t seem good, on top of there appearing to be a potentially dangerous man out there he needed to learn to protect himself against. Plus, his grandad knew something, but Arnold didn’t know where he was to talk to him. He felt like he’d had enough today. He genuinely felt that for every step forward he made, life pushed him backwards three steps. He just wanted to go home and climb into bed, unable to stomach any more disappointment for the day.

As he skulked down the corridor, Arnold contemplated simply walking past his dad’s office and going straight home. He decided against this, however, and instead made his way into his dad’s office, pushing the door open noisily to signal that he wasn’t happy.

“Woah there, what’s wrong with you?” his dad pressed. “Where’s Otto?”

“What’s a split auro?” Arnold asked, ignoring his question.

Bernard was sat at his desk, having changed back into his normal clothes. He shut his laptop and leaned forward, placing his arms on his desk. “Calm yourself and sit down. I will explain.”

“I’ll stay standing, thanks.” Arnold didn’t have a reason to be off with his dad, but he was just in a bad mood now.

“There is no need to be like that. I wouldn’t accept you talking to me like that at home and I certainly will not accept it here.”

Arnold knew his place. He walked over to the chair and sat down with his tail between his legs.

The office door swung open and as Otto entered, he gave Arnold a disapproving look before sitting down in the chair next to him.

Bernard glanced at the two of them worriedly as he shut his office door and sat down across from the boys.

"Split auros are rare, to put it frankly. Neither myself or Mr. Whittaker have ever come across one before. When an auro is split, it means that your spirit best is undecided on its form, that it is unsure on the path it needs to guide you on."

"That doesn't sound complicated," Otto replied, "even I can understand that."

"It is more getting your head around the concept," Artur continued. "A split auro means that your spirit beast doesn't know how best to guide you in times of need, Arnold, whether that be through wisdom, courage, strength, cunning, just to say a few."

"How do you know that?" Arnold asked, not fully understanding his dad's meaning.

A concerned expression came over Bernard's face, making Arnold feel even more worried.

"During the Bloodbound Ritual, your flame flickered between two forms. One was difficult to ascertain, but it indicated one possible path it could guide you down." Bernard paused, clearly uncomfortable.

"And the other?"

His dad sighed. "The other form the flame took was clearly a denotation of the dragon spirit beast. This is a darker path for you to follow. Aggression and cunning are just two of the traits shown with this type of spirit beast as well as an unforgiving anger. There has not been anyone with a known dragon spirit beast for a long time." Bernard's gaze appeared to become hazy whilst explaining this. "This isn't good, Arnold. Mr. Whittaker and the other Doyens saw this, and I have no doubt Mr. Whittaker will already be feeding back to the council that you could have a dragon inside of you." He looked worried, sweat beading on his head.

Arnold's heart began to race. This was what he had heard his dad and grandad talking about just a few nights ago, he knew it. Is this what his dad had been concerned about, that he was showing signs of a dragon spirit beast? Would this mean that he was going to walk down a darker path, that he was going to be a bad person?

"Hang on, I thought you were not allowed to tell us what the flames indicated," Otto said before Arnold had chance to. "Can you tell me mine?"

Bernard gave Otto a tired smile. "Sorry, Otto. Sometimes you need to go against what tradition tells us to do. A dragon spirit beast is not good news and I intend to make sure that you do not go down this path, Arnold. It doesn't bear thinking about." His voice broke slightly, making him appear more vulnerable than Arnold had ever seen him before. "I will be in a deep grave before I ever see my son walk down this path. I will not let something like that take you, son. A dragon spirit beast is uncontrollable."

"Don't I get a say in this? I'm a good person!" Arnold protested, confused as to why his integrity was being questioned over something totally out of his control.

"You don't understand, Arnold. For your auro to be split, it means that your spirit beast is unsure of the direction you would go when faced with difficult decisions. It doesn't know how to guide you."

"Oh," Arnold replied. He suddenly felt like he *was* a bad person, even though he hadn't actually done anything wrong.

"It's been a long evening, let's leave the Athenaeum to tomorrow. You have both had a lot to take in." Bernard began to pack up his things. "I need to try and think of a way to detract the Spirit Wardens from your split auro, but I have no doubt they will be keeping a very close eye on you. Come on, I'll drop you off too, Otto."

Whirling, anxious thoughts circled in Arnold's head all the way home. He had just accomplished something that he'd wanted his entire life. He was now an official member of the Spirit Wardens.

Yet, Arnold felt even more deflated than ever before. Now he was terrified of his spirit beast being that of the dragon, which was apparently uncontrollable and offered him a darkened and uncertain path.

But what if he could control it?

# CHAPTER 8

Arnold spent the following day feeling lethargic and specifically uninterested in everything. All he'd ever wanted was to be a Doyen and train with the Spirit Wardens like his dad had and his dad had before him. He had been given this fantastic opportunity, but he felt that the experience was ruined by learning he had a split auro.

He didn't speak a word to his parents that morning and left for school before Otto had a chance to knock on the door. Otto was just at the bottom of his street when Arnold left his house. Arnold paused for a few seconds, undecided if he was going to wait for his friend or just carry on with his walk to school by himself. He didn't know whether he was genuinely mad at Otto or just envious. He took a deep breath, then stopped to allow his friend time to catch him up. When Otto caught up to Arnold, he had a grin that spanned ear to ear, having had a much better experience with the Bloodbound Ritual than Arnold had.

"Morning, mate. I would ask how you're feeling but the fact that your face is matching the weather tells me everything."

It wasn't raining at the moment, but it had been all night. A layer of fog sat on the streets, with the skies looking particularly grey.

He was not wrong. Arnold was in a foul mood.

The two of them continued their regular journey and soon enough they were at the gates to the school. Something felt different today though. It felt like the other students were whispering and intermittently looking at the two of them as they walked past. Arnold felt his cheeks begin to glow as he blushed right on cue, a sense of paranoia overcoming him.

"Have we got our clothes on back to front or something?" Otto barked bullishly at one pupil who was pointing the two of them out to their circle of friends as they stood gossiping before form registry started. The pupil quickly diverted their attention back to their friends and avoided eye contact with Otto.

"It's rude to point," Otto said sternly as they continued to head to their form rooms.

But nothing changed as the two of them made their way through the network of hallways. Everyone was whispering to each other, some smiling at them, some looking nervously towards them as though they had three heads.

"What is going on with everyone?" Otto asked.

"It must have got out about the Spirit Wardens. Did you tell anyone?" Arnold asked.

"Not that I remember, only Everett and George know."

Arnold wanted the ground to open up and swallow him. He hated being the centre of attention, unlike Otto who didn't seem to be too bothered about everyone whispering about them. He would have just wanted to know what the gossip was.

*What if they all know about my split auro?* Arnold worried, his brain going into overdrive.

At the bottom of the hallway, they could see Everett and George talking. Everett appeared to be giving George a scolding. Arnold and Otto headed over to speak to them, knowing that they'd want to know how the previous night had gone, even though Arnold didn't feel particularly keen on explaining his split auro. When they reached the pair, Everett looked mad, and it didn't take a genius to realise who she was mad at. George hung her head, unable to look Arnold or Otto in the eyes.

"What's happening here?" Otto dove straight in, unable to subtly ask questions.

Everett stood with her arms folded. "George has something she wants to tell you."

George continued to look at the ground and began nervously moving her foot around on the floor. "I'm sorry," she stated.

Arnold had no idea why George would be apologising to them. When he saw them yesterday, everything had been fine.

She finally looked up at the two of them, only managing brief eye contact before looking down at the floor once more. "I was talking to Everett about you two joining the Spirit Wardens on our way home from school." Her tone changed as she spoke, indicating that she felt bad about something. "Well, you know, we know about the Spirit Wardens because we were invited, too. I didn't realise, well you see –"

"George!" Everett scolding her, prompting her to not go off on a tangent.

"Sorry, as I was saying . . ."

"Dawdling," Everett corrected her.

George looked at Everett and corrected herself. ". . . Talking to Everett while we were walking home, I didn't realise that Kaden was behind me along with Piers and Caleb. They heard me, and I think it is clear to see that they have told everybody about you two and the Spirit Wardens."

Arnold felt relieved that there wasn't an untrue rumour going around again like in year seven. That situation was a nightmare for Arnold, and he'd seriously considered switching schools.

Otto puffed out his chest proudly, a massive grin on his face. "We are cool," he said, ecstatic that everyone knew about them going to the Spirit Wardens.

"Don't worry, George," Arnold said. "We are really young to be allowed to join, but it was bound to get out at some point." He gave George a warm smile.

"Well, if it isn't the Spirit Wardens," a voice shouted from behind them. Arnold turned to see Kaden stood there with Piers and Caleb at either side of him. "They really are scraping the barrel with you two." Kaden had a smug grin on his face, his arms folded in front of him. Piers and Caleb sneered at them like a couple of wild jackals.

Piers stood to Kaden's left, tying his hair back, his shirt sleeves rolled up as if readying himself for a fight. He had three stud earrings in his left ear, and Arnold had heard that Piers had a tattoo but he had never seen it. To Kaden's right stood Caleb. He was taller than Kaden and was also athletically built, his mop of curly hair parting around his dark eyes.

"I took your mum out on a date last night. No hard feelings, Kaden," Otto fired back sarcastically. "Your mum's next, Piers, you don't mind, do you?"

"Funny," Kaden responded, looking unimpressed. Piers also didn't look happy, his lip curling and his knuckles white within clenched fists.

Kaden walked over and wrapped his arm around Arnold, trying to coax information out of him. "So go on, tell us all about it. What exactly are they going to do with a couple of menials anyway?"

Arnold tried to pull his head away, but Kaden had a strong grip. "There is nothing to say," Arnold said in a higher voice than he would have liked. "We are not allowed to, anyway."

"Look at that, boys. Ethon already thinks he's smarter than us."

"That's not what I meant," Arnold said defensively.

"Are you calling me thick, Ethon?"

Arnold wanted to disappear and could feel himself shrivelling up inside. "I didn't say that either."

"Come on Arnold, spill the tea!" Kaden snarled, pulling Arnold in front of him and lowering his gaze to meet his. Kaden was taller and stronger than Arnold, and the last thing Arnold wanted was to get into a fight right now.

"Leave him alone," Everett said, ramming her hand into Kaden's shoulder.

Arnold could not help but panic as the situation began to escalate, Kaden clearly incensed at Everett's intervention.

Kaden removed his arm from around Arnold and turned to face Everett. "Boar off," he sneered. Kaden looked back at Piers and Caleb and the three of them began sniggering at Everett's expense.

Everett was not taking it lying down, however. Her piercing blue eyes narrowed as she stood her ground, her gaze fixed on Kaden.

"Don't talk to her like that!" The words fell out of Arnold's mouth before he had time to think.

Kaden's gaze snapped back to Arnold, and Arnold's heart sank with the realisation of what he had just done. For someone who did not want a fight with Kaden, he had certainly antagonised the situation even more.

"Who you think you're talking to?" The thick Scottish accent from Caleb was every bit intimidating as it he intended.

Caleb and Piers walked up to Arnold and began to push him between each other.

"Did you say something?" Piers sniggered as he shoved Arnold back towards Caleb.

"Look at him, boys, he's only been at the Athenaeum once and he thinks he can take us." He pushed Arnold back. "Do you think you can take me?"

"I didn't mean anything." Arnold withdrew into himself, not

really knowing what to do. He had never gotten into trouble before, and he had never had a fight. Arnold looked at the floor, not wanting to make eye contact with either of them.

"Didn't think so. You are pathetic, Ethon," Kaden laughed. "And you've been accepted into the Spirit Wardens. Really letting their standards drop, them lot." Kaden grabbed hold of Arnold by the scruff of his shirt and struck him across his face.

A burning feeling erupted in Arnold's cheek followed by a deep throbbing as Arnold lost his footing and fell back into the wall behind him.

"Kaden, stop it!" cried Everett.

"Or?" he replied, his cockiness pouring out of him.

Suddenly Otto lunged at Kaden, pinning him against the wall. "Keep your hands off him," he growled.

Something seemed to shift in Everett. She dropped her bag from her shoulder into her hand and swung it at Piers, crashing it against his side.

Caleb ran up behind Otto and wrapped his arms around him, locking him in a bear hug. Otto pushed back, causing Caleb to lose his balance and fall onto his back with Otto landing on top of him. Arnold braced himself against the wall as he brought himself to his feet, his heart racing. He had never been in a fight before and had no idea what to do. He could hear a pulsating throb in his head and a tug of anger building in the pits of his stomach, but he swallowed this back down.

"Stop, you need to stop!" George shrieked. She was about as much of a fighter as Arnold was, and her pale complexion caused her skin to appear translucent with worry.

Piers stepped in and grabbed hold of Otto to pick him up from the floor for a beating, but a soft, purple glow materialised on the spot. Everett had summoned her boar, which now charged at Piers, knocking him off his feet.

A crowd began to form around them as pupils cheered on the fight.

Kaden clicked his neck and a dark green glow pulsated from him. He clasped his hand tightly on Everett's shoulder as a viper took form on his arm and slithered over Everett before striking at her boar that stood in front of her. As it sank its fangs into the boar's hind, Everett winced with pain, holding her side.

"Teacher!" someone yelled.

In an instant, the pulsating glow around Kaden dimmed to nothing, his spirit beast dissipating. Everett's power faded, her boar absorbing back into her, but she continued to hold her side where she'd been bitten. When she pulled her hand away, she had two small speckles of blood on her shirt.

Kaden straightened up his tie and scowled at Arnold in disgust where he sat on the floor, frozen in the situation and unaware of how to respond. "Fine example of the Spirit Wardens letting a girl do the fighting for you," he seethed.

Arnold was thankful for the fight stopping but had a feeling that the trouble with Kaden was only just beginning.

"Come on, get up before we end up off the team." Kaden helped Caleb and Piers to their feet, the latter of which had a bust lip from his tussle with Otto. "See you around, Arnold." He shoved Arnold in the shoulder, knocking him back against the wall again.

"Soon," Caleb added.

"Next time your friends won't be here to protect you," Piers finished as the three of them walked down the corridor.

Arnold felt so embarrassed by what had just happened. Why couldn't he be that bit more confident like Otto was? Arnold gathered himself and climbed to his feet, ashamed of himself for not putting up a better fight and hoping that no one else had seen what happened. His fears were realised, however, as the halls were buzzing with gossip about the scuffle that had just taken place.

Everett stood over Otto and helped him to his feet. "You

okay?" she asked, dusting his blazer down and straightening it up for him. "You held your own there."

"Thanks," he replied. "Arnold would have done the same for me. You mess with one of us, you mess with both of us."

"All of us," Everett added.

Arnold couldn't help but notice the admiration that Everett had in her eyes as she gazed at Otto, and he felt another wave of jealousy come over him. He felt he had no chance with Everett if her attentions were to turn towards his best friend.

"Are you okay?" George asked. "As soon as the fight broke out, I went to find a teacher."

Everett temporarily took her eyes from Otto as she spoke to Arnold. "Thanks for sticking up for me, too."

"You stuck up for me first," Arnold said, his eyes downcast. Today couldn't have started any worse, and it wasn't even nine o'clock. "Thanks for helping me, Otto." He was grateful for Otto's assistance, and felt annoyed at himself for his own jealousy.

The bell rang to tell them to get to their form rooms, so the four of them went their ways and headed to register for the day.

Arnold spent the rest of the day keeping to himself, avoiding all his peers and choosing to spend the breaks in solitude within the school library so that no one would bother him. By the end of the day, Arnold didn't feel like going to the Spirit Wardens, and this was only day two since completing the Bloodbound Ritual. He wished that he felt more motivated than he did, but he knew that he needed to just get his head down and get on with the training. Surely it would only be a matter of time before something positive happened.

Arnold left his final class of the day and headed to the front of the school to wait for Otto. To his surprise, Otto was already waiting for him, which was very uncharacteristic of him.

"In a rush?" Arnold felt able to muster some sarcastic humour despite his mood.

"Excited to learn more. Last night was the best experience I have ever had." Otto's enthusiasm was all over his face. "I want to get stuck into the work that we have been set and find out what our spirit beasts are going to be." He paused for a moment, noticing that Arnold was nowhere near as excited as he was. "I know you're annoyed about yesterday, but let's just give it a try and see how we get on with the Spirit Wardens tonight."

Arnold admired Otto's enthusiasm and appreciated him trying to encourage him to give things another try. For his own sanity, he decided that he would not ruin the evening by being moody all night. "I'll try and be more positive," he pledged.

As the two walked through the front door to the Spirit Wardens, they were greeted by a smiling Raine.

"Good evening, boys, how are you both today?" Her smile was infectious and instantly made Arnold feel welcome. Some of his apprehension and anxiety lifted.

"How do we get to the library?" Otto asked eagerly, without greeting her. Otto wasn't exactly known for his manners.

"Hi," Arnold said, "Please could you tell us where the library is? Mr. Whittaker has set us a task to complete." He wondered where his dad might be as he spoke with Raine, thinking that he would have been there to greet the two of them.

Raine smiled again and pointed. "If you follow the hallway here, you can't miss it. You will both need to register your fingerprints with me first so I can grant you access." She waved the two of them over to her desk.

"You first, Arnold. Please just put your index finger on the pressure pad in front of you until I say." She tapped her hand on the small device that was fixed into the desk. The glass covering was a dark red colour, and Arnold could see the mixed fingerprints from other people that must have been registered before them.

Arnold placed his index finger as directed by Raine on the small device and after a short while, the device let out a short beep.

"You can take your finger off now. Otto, please, can you do the same."

Otto placed his finger down and again a short beep sounded, indicating that Raine had registered his fingerprint.

"Mr. Whittaker has given you access to the library for now. This is the only area of the Athenaeum you have access to until you are told otherwise by Mr. Whittaker." Raine spoke with efficiency as thought the three of them were in a business meeting. "Until then, this is the only area you are permitted to enter on your own." She pointed down the hallway again. "When you get there, place your finger against the device by the door. This will grant you access." Raine looked back down at her desk and began to write something down in the diary that was next to the phone.

"Make sure you follow Mr. Whittaker's orders. He is one for rules and I don't think he would miss an opportunity to reprimand you both."

Arnold and Otto nodded, then made their way down the hallway until they reached large, frosted double doors. As Raine had told them, to the right of the door was the same type of device as at the front desk where they had registered their fingerprints. Otto placed his index finger on the red glass in the centre of the device, and after a few seconds, the familiar bleep from the device sounded and the frosting from the glass vanished in an instant. A few seconds later, the doors slid open, granting the two of them access. Arnold stepped through the doorway and was taken aback at the expense that must have gone into this room. There were multiple rows of books running the length of the chamber from floor to ceiling. In the centre of the room stood a screen fixed into a tabletop.

"Woah," Arnold gasped. This was like no library he had ever seen before.

Otto had already made his way to the glowing screen in the centre of the room. As much as Arnold liked reading books, Otto was the complete opposite and preferred to use technology to improve his knowledge.

Arnold gazed around the room trying to take in the detail, from the intricate tiled floor to the impressive carvings that were individual to each row of bookshelves lining the Athenaeum.

"This makes it miles easier," Otto said, beckoning Arnold to come look at the screen with him.

Arnold walked across the room to see what the fuss was about.

"Looks like you can type in what you're looking for and it will tell us where to look. This will be easy." There was a smugness about Otto. "We will have our first task completed in no time. I can't wait to find out what our spirit beasts are."

He typed in 'big cats', but the screen let out a loud noise to indicate that the search had been denied.

Arnold laughed, knowing that it would not have been that easy. "Looks like it's blocked."

"What now?" Otto asked.

"We do this the old-fashioned way." Arnold looked out at the vast expanse of books within the room and felt daunted himself. He knew he needed to find anything on spirit beasts that could fly, but had no clue where to start within the Athenaeum.

"Bugger," Otto sighed. He wasn't as patient as Arnold.

Arnold walked to the front row of books and began looking at the first shelf to see what order the books were in, but he was stumped; they were not in alphabetical order, nor were they categorised by author, size, or topic.

"Sack this," Otto shouted. "Someone has mixed all these up, this doesn't make any sense."

"Going to have to look at these one at a time until we find something that means something for us." Arnold felt more upbeat than Otto, but he knew that this was going to take some time to achieve. Being around books brought Arnold a level of comfort that he could not explain. Books had always been his way of escaping.

He started to pull out the books from the shelf in no particular order. One was on the history of Oswaldtwistle which he promptly put back onto the shelf.

*This is going to take forever*, he thought to himself. Looking across at Otto, he couldn't help but laugh out loud at his utterly bemused expression, as if he were horrified at the prospect of actually having to read a book. Otto stood with his hands on his hips, looking up at the books but not being proactive enough to reach out and grab one.

Arnold began to walk slowly down the aisle, choosing to focus on the top shelf of books. He took care to read the titles of each one as he walked past. Once he had gotten to the bottom of the first aisle, he began to walk back, this time focusing on the next step down. Skimming over the titles, he saw author's such as P.A. Bartholomew, Nathanial Rind, and Betsy Devon. He pulled one of the books out by P.A. Bartholomew, which had a picture of a woodland on the front, the title of the book in bold yellow letters reading, *The Origins of Insectoid Spirit Beasts*. Arnold put it down and picked up another titled, *Examining the Concept of Spirit Beasts: A Dive Through History*. On the front of the cover was the image of a dolphin, its spirit beast power flowing around it. Arnold found himself straining a yawn simply reading the book titles, let alone skimming them. He couldn't see anything meaningful for himself or Otto so he placed the book back down to continue searching.

After around twenty minutes of this process, Arnold

announced to Otto, "I think it's safe to say this first row of books is about history. Have you found anything interesting yet?"

"No, haven't got a clue what I am looking at here. Doesn't seem to be anything on big cat spirit beasts." He paused, something seeming to catch his eye. "Oh, hang on, think I might have something up there." Otto appeared confused as he looked around the room.

"What's wrong?"

"How am I meant to get it down? There's no ladders in here." Otto seemed frustrated at the lack of tools available for them to complete their task. "Don't let me forget that that book is up there, I'll come back to that later."

Over the next few days, Arnold and Otto spent their evenings after school in the Athenaeum, trying their hardest to find specific books around groups and types of spirit animals, but so far they had found none. Arnold thought the process was quite therapeutic, and he quickly fell into a steady routine of systematically making his way through the vast archive, making note of the different categories he discovered along the way.

"This is like being in prison," Otto cried after four days of searching through the library after school. "This is so unhelpful."

"You're not being forced to be here."

"I know that, I'm just saying."

But Arnold was growing discouraged. They'd managed to check every row of books, yet still hadn't found anything that could be of any use to them. He was starting to feel like they'd been sent on a fool's errand, but Mr. Whittaker had made it clear that they could not progress until this task had been successfully completed.

"Right, I've had enough," Otto said impatiently. He had begun pacing the large wall of books on the far side of the Athenaeum. "I'm getting that book up there." He pointed at the book he was certain would contain information on big cats, even though it was too high up for him to read it. "Can you use your super sight to see up there?"

Kicking himself for not having thought of this earlier, Arnold focused in the direction that Otto was pointing, and true to form, he could see the names of the books clearly. Otto had been right all along; there was a book up there that looked like it could be about big cats, titled *Spirit Beasts of Africa*. Looking at the books just above these, Arnold realised that it was the upper section of the wall that contained the books they'd been looking for all along. Judging by the various titles, they seemed to be specifically about spirit beasts.

"You were right," Arnold informed him. "How do we get to them, though?"

Arnold looked around the room, but there was no sign of anything that the two of them would be able to use to scale the wall of books and reach the section they so clearly needed.

"Come here," Otto demanded. "I've got an idea. Stand by that wall."

Arnold did as he was asked and walked towards the corner of the room, uncertain what Otto had planned for him.

"I'm going to face the wall," Otto told him. "You need to climb up on my shoulders. Then I'll shimmy across the wall to where the book is, and you grab it. You can use the window ledge there to pull yourself up on my shoulders."

Arnold felt that the idea was doomed to fail, but Otto had the athletic build now to be able to carry his weight if he were to climb onto his shoulders. But would he be able to move around with him up there? Arnold didn't exactly love the prospect of sustaining another concussion if he fell, but he wasn't really seeing any other option at this point. Furthermore, he didn't want to be forced to report to Mr. Whittaker that they'd been unable to complete their first assignment as official members of the Spirit Wardens.

Otto crouched down onto the floor, positioning himself so that Arnold could climb into his shoulders. Arnold placed one foot onto Otto's shoulder and pushed himself up from the ground. As his momentum took him upwards, he grabbed hold of the window ledge to keep himself balanced.

"That wasn't too bad, was it?" Otto grinned. "Okay, don't fall." He began to slowly push himself from the ground to stand up. It was a good job it was Otto underneath, as Arnold would not have been able to do this if their positions were reversed. Otto kept his hands against the wall in front of him to keep his balance, and Arnold shifted his hands from the window ledge to the face of the wall. A sense of panic overcame him. He felt very vulnerable now, as he had nothing to hold onto. Otto managed to get his legs fully extended and stepped slowly sideways until the pair of them became level with the wall of books. Arnold quickly started reading the side covers of the books to find the one that Otto wanted, knowing that they wouldn't be able to maintain this position for long.

Arnold realised that they were still not tall enough, as the book remained just out of his reach.

"I can't reach it," he told Otto, "I'm still not high enough."

"Great, hang on." Otto shuffled his feet and began to push his shoulders up, standing on his tiptoes. He let out a grunt as the strain from Arnold standing on him began to set in.

Keeping his arm outstretched, Arnold could just reach the bottom of the book but not enough for him to grab it. He felt himself lower once more as Otto was forced to plant his feet, the strenuous task beginning to tire him.

"I can't keep you there much longer, you're going to have to hurry up," Otto panted. "I think I've got one more try in me. Hold on." He pushed up on to his tiptoes again, attempting to get Arnold as high up as possible.

Arnold reached for the book again but was still struggling. He pulled out the two books next to it and dropped them behind him. The book he wanted then fell towards him into the gap he had created, finally allowing him to grab hold of it. He then glimpsed the title of a book beyond it that caught his attention: *Dragons, Birds, and Dreams.*

That was too much of a coincidence.

"Hang on, there's another book here that I need."

"Hurry up."

Arnold reached out as far as he could but lost his footing, sliding from Otto's shoulders. He fell sideways, taking out multiple shelves in the wall as he fell to the floor. He heard a crunching noise as he slammed to the floor, realising it was Otto underneath him. There was an almighty crash as book after book began to fall from the wall and land on top of them. When the books eventually stopped falling, the two of them let out loud groans.

Arnold was certain he was going to have some pretty bad bruises. "My dad is going to kill me," he said, realising the trouble the two of them would be in for the mess they had caused.

"Never mind that, Mr. Whittaker is going to go mental. Did you get the book I needed and can you get off me?" a muffled voice came from underneath Arnold.

Arnold pushed the books off him and rolled to his side before climbing back to his feet, then turned to help Otto free himself from the books.

The two of them stood there looking at the pile of books on the floor.

"Job done, that will make it easier for us," Otto said whilst dusting himself down. "Winner." He picked up the book that he had asked Arnold to grab off the floor. "I'll be over there with this." He walked off, leaving Arnold staring at the pile of books on the floor before him.

Arnold needed to find that book. He dropped to his knees and began removing the books one at a time, the task becoming more laborious with every time that he moved. Soon, Arnold felt like giving up; it was like searching for a needle in a haystack.

Sighing in frustration, he got to his feet, realising it was futile. But then something caught his eye. Excitedly, Arnold plucked a partially buried book from the pile, a rare smile finding its way to his face. *Dragons, Birds, and Dreams.* He'd found it!

Finally, something positive.

A feeling of accomplishment engulfed him as he clutched the book in his hands, eager to discover what lay within. When Arnold glanced at the pile again, he spotted an open book with a picture on one of the pages that looked familiar to him. He picked this one up as well to examine it closer.

On the open page was a drawing of a dagger that had intricate inscriptions within the blade and the handle. Staring at the picture, it dawned on Arnold where he had seen this dagger before. It was from the evening of Arnold's birthday when they saved the old Doyen. The scarred man had this blade, Arnold was sure of it. His heart racing, Arnold skimmed the text, and what he learned only confirmed his suspicions even more. The black hilt was described as being made of ebony, and the blade itself had been created from rare ivory taken from an elephant spirit beast. Arnold stared at the picture, taking in every detail he could from the carvings in the peculiar shape of the handle and the blade. He turned the book over to see what the book was titled: *Ancient Artefacts of the Spirit Realm*, by Betsy Devon. Arnold had never heard of her before, and he considered himself well-read when it came to spirit beast literature.

"Otto, come here, you need to see this!" Arnold showed him the page with the diagram of the dagger.

Otto took a look but didn't appear to see what Arnold was seeing.

"He had this blade that night," Arnold said. "The scarred man has this dagger!"

"I never saw his dagger. Are you sure?"

"Definitely," Arnold replied.

"The Blade of the Spirits?" Otto said, reading out loud over Arnold's shoulder.

Arnold turned the page to see if there was any more information on the blade, and there was. He began to recite the paragraph:

*13th April 1951*

*This investigation had proven nothing but troublesome from start to finish. After spending eleven months searching for the Blade of the Spirits, we had all but given up. That was, until we received a new lead from an anonymous source about an ancient temple that could hold the answers we were looking for. Following the directions we received, we eventually found the ancient ruins after a month of searching. We entered the temple with high hopes of finally securing this ancient artefact, and to our joy, it was there on an overgrown pedestal. We are in the process of translating the hieroglyphs which denote two giant mane-less lions. Could it be that this blade is the one that controls the lions of the Aether? If our findings are correct, then somehow the two giant spirit beasts can be controlled by whoever holds the blade. There are more hieroglyphs left to translate which we are eagerly awaiting feedback for.*

*This is the blade that we need for the ceremony, this is the blade we need to save my best friend.*

*-Betsy Devon*

Arnold turned to the next page to see pictures of the glyphs that Betsy Devon had spoken about, and true to her words, they resembled ancient carvings that depicted two mane-less lions. He re-read the paragraph, wanting to take in as much information as possible. He passed the book to Otto so that he could read the pages, too.

Otto scratched his head. "What's the lions of the Aether?"

Arnold's excitement was mounting. "I don't know, but I want to find out." Feeling re-invigorated, he made for the door, anxious to speak with his dad about what they had discovered. He felt certain that this information would be crucial for the investigation into the scarred man and wanted to report it as soon as possible.

"Where do you think you are going?" Mr. Whittaker stood at the doorway of the Athenaeum, looking severely unimpressed at the mess that had been mad.

"We need to –"

"What you *need* to do, Mr. Ethon, is leave this room in the condition that you found it in," Mr. Whittaker snapped, cutting Arnold off mid-sentence. He walked over to the screen that was in the centre of the room and began to press the keypad. Next to the double doors, a cupboard opened that neither boys had noticed before. Within it sat a set of ladders.

Without a word, Mr. Whittaker turned and stalked out of the room, the double doors sliding shut behind him.

"As if the ladders were there all along, that's so annoying," Otto vented.

"Yeah, but we wouldn't have found this if we'd know about the ladders," Arnold replied. He clutched the book with the drawings of the dagger to his chest. He planned to read this in its entirety.

## CHAPTER 9

Two hours later, Arnold and Otto exited the library and made their way back to the reception area, where they found Raine packing up to finish for the day.

She switched off her computer and stood up to put her long, light pink coat on. "Have you boys all finished? I'm not going to lie, you were both very entertaining on the CCTV." She chuckled to herself as she picked her bag up and slung it over her shoulder. Arnold immediately felt his cheeks grow hot.

"If you're looking for your dad, he is in his office waiting to take you both home. I will see you both on Monday. Have a nice weekend!" She waved at them as she walked through the front door, and the boys headed to Bernard's office, remembering their way from the first time they had arrived at the Spirit Wardens.

Without knocking, Arnold burst into his dad's office. "I've found something, Dad!" he exclaimed, not wanting to waste any time.

Bernard looked a bit exasperated as if he wanted to scold Arnold for his lack of manners, but seemed to change his mind. "About your spirit beast?" he replied instead.

"It's about the scarred man," Otto declared.

"The scarred man? How?"

Arnold placed the book on his dad's desk, opening it to the page with the drawing of the dagger.

Bernard studied the picture for a short while before lifting his head to look at Arnold expectantly. "What is this?" he asked.

"It's the blade that I saw that night! This was the blade that the scarred man had," Arnold proclaimed.

"Are you sure?" his dad fired back. "Let me see that." He grabbed the book and flicked through the pages.

"I'm sure of it, Dad, that's the blade he was carrying."

"If this is true, then he is in possession of an ancient artefact."

"I know what I saw. I saw this blade in his hands. I saw him trying to absorb Charles's spirit beasts with it." Arnold turned the pages over to the paragraph he had read. "What are the lions of the Aether?"

"The lions of the Aether?" Bernard questioned.

"Yes, read that paragraph," Arnold said, pointing. "Betsy Devon mentions them."

Bernard was silent for a moment as he read the journal entry. "It's a true story," he said when he had finished. "Well, part of it is. You see, there are many myths about the lions of the Aether, but they were never found to be true."

Arnold and Otto sat down on the chairs opposite his dad's desk, both completely drawn in to the conversation and both equally fascinated by what they were about to be told.

Bernard began to go into detail around what he knew. "The lions of the Aether were two man-hunting lions said to have terrorised workers who were building a new railway line in Africa in the late 1800s. These lions were larger than usual, more powerful, and so the stories say, they were spirit beasts untethered to a human anchor."

"That's pretty cool." Otto's eyes were wide as he listened intently to the story.

Bernard continued, "It wasn't cool. At the time, this was terrifying for the workers. The Spirit Wardens had to work closely with our overseas counterparts to find them and hunt them down. Between March and December, it was estimated that they had killed over a hundred workers on the railway line. These lions were clever and did not fall for any traps that were set to capture them. They stalked their prey like they knew who they wanted to kill. They were eventually hunted and killed by Hugo Wrean, one of the lead Spirit Wardens who was tasked with finding the beasts."

"And the theory?" Arnold pressed, eager to know the rest of the story.

"There was a rumour that the lions were under the control of a soul-weaver who was using a dagger that he had enchanted. Not happy with the railway line being built, he wanted to stop it from progressing by targeting the workers. After the lions were killed, it was said that the soul-weaver took the spirits of these animals and transferred them to a blade where they were to be harboured, granting their wielder the ability to summon them. But it's just a story," Bernard finished, waving his hand dismissively.

"They could be summoned, like a spirit beast?" Arnold asked, undeterred.

"Yes. No one knows where the dagger went after that – assuming it was ever real in the first place – so as I said, this is just a myth."

"Until now," Otto countered. "That is, if the scarred man really does have the dagger."

"He does," Arnold insisted, positive that he was not mistaken.

Arnold's dad appeared sceptical, however, and stood up from behind his desk. "We need more evidence. Mr. Whittaker will not go off a hunch."

"But Dad, I know what I saw."

"Sorry, Arnold, we need more proof before we can do anything. I'm not saying I don't believe you, but I know how Mr. Whittaker works, and he will want some evidence." Bernard began to tidy his desk. "Come on, boys it's getting late now. Let's head back."

Arnold felt the frustration building in him again, wishing that his dad would just take his word. It seemed to him that it didn't matter what he did or said, his dad would always find some way of casting doubt over what he was doing or thinking.

Feeling dejected, Arnold withdrew into himself, choosing not to engage in any further conversation. He picked up his schoolbag from the floor and tucked the old book along with the book about dragons and birds inside it knowing he would spend the rest of the night reading as much as possible.

"You okay?" Otto asked, knowing that Arnold wouldn't be happy with his dad.

"I'll be fine, getting used to it now." Arnold slung his bag over his shoulder and began to follow his dad from his office down to the car park. The three of them entered the car and Arnold's dad set off towards Otto's house to drop him first, an awkward silence filling the vehicle as Arnold sat in the front seat, choosing to stare out the window in an attempt to avoid eye contact.

The story of the lions of the Aether running through his head, Arnold began to wonder, if the story were true, how a dagger could control the two beasts. If a soul-weaver had been involved, was it possible to create such a powerful artefact? Arnold knew that soul-weavers had the ability to create artefacts, but he didn't know if there were any soul-weavers around anymore. They were rarely spoken of, and he was under the impression they had faded away with history.

Theirs was a practice that was unheard of nowadays. It was incredibly rare for someone to be able to connect to the spirit world in the way that they could, and rarer still to be able to harness their energy and transfer it to items of their choosing. In the old days, spirit-weavers used weapons and trinkets for that very purpose.

Before long, the car pulled up outside Otto's house.

"Thanks," Otto commented before shutting the door and heading through his front door. Arnold nodded towards him, and his dad waved from behind the steering wheel before setting off. The awkward silence hung heavy in the car.

"I didn't say I didn't believe you," Bernard said softly after a time. "I just said we needed more evidence to back up what you were saying. You can't fall out with me every time I give you advice."

Arnold knew that although his dad was trying to support him, he was also receiving a ticking off at the same time.

"Sorry, Dad, it's been a long week."

"Tell me about it. We have nothing on the scarred man, not a single lead. He has literally vanished into thin air."

A tune began playing through the car speakers and the dashboard lit up to say that Mr. Whittaker was ringing. Arnold's dad answered the call.

"Bernard, stop whatever you are doing and head to the hospital," Mr. Whittaker's hurried voice echoed throughout the car. "Mr. Grey has woken up."

"Sir, I have Arnold with me –"

"Take the boy with you, he can wait in reception. You won't be there long, and I need you there now."

"Yes, sir," Bernard replied.

"Call me as soon as you have seen him."

Bernard diverted from the route they were taking and began to drive in the direction of the hospital. After around fifteen minutes they had arrived at the infirmary, and Bernard pulled up by the side car park.

"Ridiculous that I have to pay for the parking when I'm working," he grumbled.

The two of them left the car and made their way to the entrance of the hospital. As they walked through the large, glass automatic doors, Arnold was faced with the mixed smells of antiseptic and cleaning products, which gave the air a distinct fragrance that he associated with hospitals.

"Here's some money for a drink and the vending machine, get yourself something if you need to." Bernard reached into his pocket and pulled out a handful of change and placed it in Arnold's hand. "I shouldn't be too long, maybe around half an hour."

Bernard turned around and headed off down the hospital corridor in the general direction of the ward where Mr. Grey must have been.

Arnold sat in the waiting area and examined each person that was sat around him, trying to figure out the different reasons people may be there. There was the man in his row that looked like he may have a broken arm, a toddler with an egg on their head where they must have bumped themselves, and an elderly couple that Arnold couldn't quite figure out which one was waiting to be seen. The antiseptic fragrance continued to engulf his nose and he couldn't decide whether he liked it or hated it.

Another ten minutes passed, and Arnold decided that he wanted a drink and a packet of crisps from the vending machine.

On his way back to his seat, Arnold was surprised to spot a familiar face come into the reception area. It was his grandad.

Elwood walked over to the receptionist before heading off down the same corridor that Bernard had gone down.

*What's he doing here?* Arnold thought to himself. They had so much to discuss.

Taking a big gulp of his pop, Arnold threw this in the bin before shoving the crisp packet into his pocket. He set off walking down the corridor and rounded the corner just in time to see his grandad turn right. Arnold quickly followed, and when he got to the bottom of the hallway, he saw his grandad turn left.

Arnold didn't have a clue where he was going, and realised that if he lost him, he most likely would need to ask for directions to get back to the main reception area. He wasn't even sure he was supposed to be back here.

Arnold continued to follow his grandad, fighting the urge to shout out to him. He worried that his grandad would make him go back and wait in the reception, but his presence had piqued Arnold's curiosity, and he wanted to know what was going on.

Arnold walked past the edge of the next corridor to see his grandad walk into a ward.

*Who is he here to see?* Arnold wondered. It was clear by the way his grandad kept glancing around that he did not want his presence here known. What was he hiding?

Intrigued, Arnold again followed, but the auto lock on the doors had just kicked in as he reached them, stopping him from going any further. Arnold was wondering what to do next when he saw a cleaner pushing a trolley coming towards him on the other side of the double doors. She pressed a button on the other side and the doors unlocked.

"Can I help you?" she asked as Arnold tried to walk past her.

"Sorry, I'm here to see my grandad," he replied, happy knowing that he hadn't really lied to her.

"Okay then, go on." She pushed her trolley through the door and allowed Arnold to pass.

"Thank you," Arnold said politely, then walked down another corridor looking down each bay of beds to try and find where his grandad had gone. He was walking past a closed-off room when he heard his grandad's muffled voice.

Arnold moved closer to try and hear what was being said.

"How are you, Charles?" his grandad spoke with concern.

"You had me worried, enough to meet with the others. They send their best."

"I'm not going to lie, Elwood, I have felt better," a croaked, weary voice replied. "How are you? It has been far too long."

Arnold moved his position to look through the glass panel in the window. His grandad and his dad stood on either side of a bed. He could see Charles sat up with a dinner table slid in front of him.

The atmosphere in the room appeared to change as the old man began to speak about his attack. "That man, he knew who I was, and he knew that I used to be a Doyen, I am sure of it!" His voice became slightly agitated. "He had the dagger, Elwood, he had the Blade of the Spirits."

His grandad stepped back from Charles. "Are you absolutely certain? You're saying someone attacked you using it? That can't be possible, that blade is gone."

"I know exactly when that blade went missing, I was there with you," Charles volleyed back. "I think he knows what we did."

"That's impossible. There were four of us there, and your Betsy is no longer with us."

"Don't you mean five?" Charles corrected.

"Arnold spoke of the blade," Bernard said. "He found a picture in a book from the Athenaeum's library, and was adamant that your attacker had it. He was right." Bernard sounded surprised.

Arnold took a sense of satisfaction from knowing that he had been right around the blade that he seen, but now had more questions than ever. He now knew there was a link between his grandad, Charles, and the man with the Blade of the Spirits, but he had no idea why that man would have attacked Charles. His grandad had said they spent a long time looking for the blade, so the two of them must have worked together as Doyens years ago. Arnold began to feel concerned about his grandad. If the man had attacked Charles with the blade, surely there was a possibility that he could also come after his grandad.

Charles's face was pale, as if all the blood had been drained from him. "You don't think that she –"

There was a loud bang at the auto lock doors that Arnold had walked through to enter the ward. The force was thunderous, and Arnold could swear he felt the floor rumble underneath his feet. This was quickly followed by another loud bang and another. As he looked down the corridor, he could see dust and what he hoped was not debris from the ceiling raining onto the polished floor. After two more loud bangs, Arnold heard the auto lock doors swing open, smashing into the walls on either side. There was silence for a few seconds, followed by a scream from one a woman further down towards the airlock. This was greeted by a deafening roar that shook Arnold to the bone. Fear overcoming him, he stepped back from the door.

He had heard this roar before, the night they rescued Charles. He looked down the corridor to see a large, spectral lion running at speed down the corridor towards him, its giant muscular frame covered with scars from its previous battles. Wisps of orange spectral energy curled and danced around it, a ghostly auro that seemed to blur the boundary between physical and ethereal. The energy pulsated with life, not merely a haze but a cascading shroud of otherworldly power that held an almost tangible substance.

Arnold tried to move out of the way, but the large spirit beast crashed into him, sending him flying through the air and into the nurse's station in the middle of the ward. Arnold winced as he hit the edge of the desk and landed back on the floor. Dazed, he looked up to see the lion run straight past him. Arnold could hear the muffled screams of the other patients and the staff members on the ward as he gathered himself. All he could see were legs running past him as everyone ran away from the sound of the growling lion, its supernatural glow lighting up the ward. Arnold pulled himself to his knees, searching over at the door where he knew Charles, his grandad, and dad were. Past the door, he could see a crowd of people scrambling to get away from the lion.

That's when he saw him.

The man walked slowly through the crowd, uninterested in the people running past him, his bone dagger clenched tightly in his hand. He walked down the corridor with a sense of calm, his gaze moving from one bay to the next as he scanned the area.

Arnold froze in place, staying crouched down in position and hoping the man wouldn't see him. The scarred man, however, stopped in his tracks when he noticed Arnold. Arnold pulled himself up unsteadily against the nurse station.

"You," the man growled. "Luckily, I am not here for you." He had stopped in front of Charles's hospital room. "Maybe after I am done with the old man, I will make you pay for the inconvenience you have caused."

The door to Charles's room kicked open and Arnold's dad threw himself at the scarred man, knocking him into the wall.

"Go!" he shouted as Arnold's grandad exited the room with Charles draped over his shoulder.

Arnold was impressed by the ease with which his grandad appeared to be carrying Charles. Elwood began to make his way towards the broken autolock doors at the entrance to the ward. Arnold panicked when he realised that his dad had not seen him, and had no idea he was on the ward. He tried to call out but was still winded from the lion running into him, and no words fell from his mouth.

"You won't stop me," the scarred man seethed, staring into Bernard's dark eyes. Bernard challenged him with a stern gaze of his own. The man launched into action, pushing back against Bernard before freeing an arm and striking him across the face. He attempted to strike again, but Bernard blocked this and aimed a blow into the man's midriff, who let out a gasp of air as he made contact. He looked infuriated, his eyes bulging as he pushed Bernard back with considerable force, knocking him backwards into the wall behind him. The attacker then let loose with a flurry of blows, with Bernard just managing to block the odd one before he was struck in the head. He fell to the floor, and the stranger grabbed him by his clothes before throwing him at the opposite wall where he lay motionless, unconscious from the attack. The scarred man turned and began to walk in the direction that Elwood had fled with Charles.

"Come!" he shouted out loudly, and Arnold instantly realised who he was talking to.

Loud, inhuman footsteps farther down the hallway began to steadily get faster. Arnold knew he needed to do something to help his grandad and Charles, to buy them some time. Thinking fast, he hopped over the nurse's station and tried to push the desk out into the corridor, but the weight of it was making it difficult. Realising he didn't have long, he turned and pushed his back against it, bracing his legs against the wall and pushing the desk with as much strength as he could muster. Arnold's muscles burned as he attempted to move the station, and finally he could feel it budge. A light-blue glow of energy sprung up around him.

With a thud, the lion crashed into the desk, knocking it farther down the corridor and sending Arnold falling to the floor. Lying on his back, Arnold started to panic. He could hear the breathing of the lion as it prowled the area. His heart raced as he desperately thought of what to do next. Arnold knew he wouldn't be able to fight off the lion on his own if it attacked.

Climbing to his feet as fast as he could, he surveyed the area searching for the man with the blade, who was now out of sight. To his horror, the exit route was blocked by the upturned nurse's station, which left him stranded in the ward with the giant lion. Panicked, Arnold jumped backwards to create some distance between him and the lion which he realised was still lying on the floor after its collision with the nurse's station. But the lion was beginning to gather itself, and as a low grumble of dissatisfaction emanated dangerously from its throat, Arnold's chest tightened. He tried to steady his breathing, placing his hand over his mouth to quieten himself so that the lion wouldn't realise he was still there.

Spotting some more doors with a fire escape light above it, he glanced over at the lion and realised it was getting to its feet. He was out of time.

Arnold snuck towards the fire escape, trying his hardest to do this as silently as he could. He hoped that his dad was okay, as the lion couldn't get past the upturned desk without forcing it. He crept towards the fire exit in front of him, keeping the lion to his left.

Then another low grumbling noise erupted from his right, disorienting Arnold. His adrenaline spiked, and he could hear his own heartbeat as his blood pumped around his body at an elevated rate. His legs felt ready to give way under him, his whole body shaking with fear.

Standing by a large window at the top of the ward was a second lion of the same size. Ethereal flames flickered and licked at the air around the creature, casting an unearthly glow that reflected in its eyes. Arnold's heart sank. The lion had its eyes firmly fixed on him as if he were the prey it was hunting.

*How do you outrun a lion?*

Arnold's mind raced with every scenario he faced, and none of them ended well for him.

The lion let out a blood-curdling roar that almost knocked Arnold's legs from underneath him, filling him with dread to his core. He set off at pace and made for the fire escape, his legs feeling as though the bones had been removed and replaced with jelly. The lion gave chase as Arnold slammed his hands against the metal bar of the door, which burst open in front of him. He ran as fast as he could down the concrete steps two at a time. When he reached the bottom of the first row of steps, he risked a glance up at the door just as the lion leapt through the air towards him, clearing all the steps with ease.

Arnold continued to run down the next row of steps as the lion smashed into the wall behind him, barely missing him. It was so close that he could feel the heat of its breath, or maybe it was the heart of its power from the spirit world.

Arnold reached the bottom again as the lion cleared the next row of steps, and this time Arnold just managed to roll out of the way as the lion thumped against the wall. He knew he needed to think fast, but he needed to move even faster. Seeing no other option, Arnold grabbed hold of the rail, the cold steel sending an icy chill into his hands.

*This is mad*, he thought.

He gathered himself and took a deep breath, then climbed over the railing, dropping to the floor below. The sensation of weightlessness came over him for a brief moment before he went crumpling into the floor with a sickening thud. He let out a gasp as the air inside him exited instantly. He pulled himself up using the railing and a sharp sting erupted in his ankle. The throbbing pain travelled far up his leg, and nausea gripped the back of his throat.

Hearing the lion jump down the next row of stairs, Arnold knew he had no option but to do the same again. He rolled over the top of the railings again just as the lion drew level with him, its outstretched claw barely missing him. He slammed into the floor again, landing on his side. Tasting iron in his mouth, he spat a small amount of blood onto the dirty, concrete floor, his mouth throbbing. The wind was well and truly knocked out of him, and he instantly knew that this time he had done something to his arm. Searing pain traced from his shoulder downwards, pain like he had never felt before. He needed to get back to his feet quickly, otherwise the lion would be upon him.

Dazed, dizzy, and in an immense amount of pain, Arnold felt he had nothing left. His energy was drained, his body broken.

*Get up, Arnold. Get up and get through those doors.* His inner voice guided him, and from somewhere he plucked up the will and strength to continue.

He had made it to the ground floor. Arnold fought against every muscle in his body to stand up, somehow managing to muster enough strength to climb to his feet once more.

*Move!* he told himself.

Limping heavily, he made his way towards the emergency exit, tasting iron. The world spun around him, and he struggled to keep his balance as his legs began to give way, feeling as they were glued to the ground. Exhausted, he threw himself as hard as he could against the exit door, forcing it open. He fell through it onto the solid gravel outside.

Arnold rolled onto his back in agony and with no energy left. He had never felt anything like the fear and pain that he was currently experiencing. His heart continued to race as he thought about what to do next. He was fresh out of ideas.

Lying in the darkness, Arnold could hear the soft rumble of the lion as it made its way slowly outside. It was calm, collected, it was stalking him, it was hunting him. Its eyes fixed on Arnold as it crouched and started to crawl towards him, ready to strike.

Arnold closed his eyes, bracing himself for a blow that surely would mean the end of him.

His pulsating fear was interrupted by a loud roar which filled the air, shaking Arnold to his bones. This roar, however, sounded different from the lion's. He opened his eyes to see a bear smash into the side of the spectral lion, knocking it off its feet. The bear, coated in a dark blue energy, continued its charge and ran at the lion, standing on its back legs to strike the lion with considerable force. The lion growled as the grizzly bear bored into its side. The lion snapped back, with the bear quickly jumping back to its feet. The lion stood and let out a thunderous roar which the bear greeted with its equally deafening battle cry. The two of them bared their razor-sharp teeth towards each other.

Leaping through the air with its intensely muscular legs, the lion landed on the bear and sunk its knife-like teeth into its back. The bear let out a groaning noise as it attempted to shake it off.

The light emitting from the two spirit beasts illuminated the environment around them, but Arnold was unable to see outside the periphery, the rest of his surroundings lost to the shadows.

He had never seen the grizzly bear spirit beast like this, so ferocious and fierce, but was sure that it was his dads. The darkened blue energy that glowed around it matched his dad's auro. The awe-inspiring beast was more than holding its own against the giant, mane-less lion. The orange energy of the lion as well as the blue of the bear led to a swirling blur of colours as the two beasts continued to grapple with each other, both trading blows with one another with their huge, shovel-like paws. Claws drawn, they continued to swipe at each other's heads, with the bear looking as if it was beginning to get the upper hand.

The second lion exited the building, making its way into the battle. It began to run at speed to protect its brother.

"The second one's there!" Arnold screamed, trying to alert the bear, but it was too late. Within seconds, the second lion had run into the fracas and lunged at the grizzly, clawing it all the way down its back. The bear let out an ear-piercing roar and the two lions began to pummel it, their claws piercing the spectral animal's thick natural armour as if shredding paper.

The bear tried in vain to fight back, its wounds from the

battle taking their toll. One of the lions jumped towards it, with the bear managing to bite the lion and use its momentum to throw it past him. However, as it did this, the other lion was quickly upon it, slamming its body into the bear's head and knocking it to the floor. Sensing the bear's fading power, the two lions crouched down, staring at the grizzly bear and waiting to pounce.

Arnold lay there feeling tense, injured, and unable to do anything to help. He felt completely powerless. The lions were now teasing the bear, dragging out their final attack and causing Arnold to feel even more anxious and useless.

But the final blow never came. Suddenly, the two lions stood up and ran off into the field next to the hospital, the light glow around them becoming smaller and smaller as they vanished into the distance. Arnold had no idea what had set them off, but he didn't care.

He could hear a low grumble emitting from the grizzly bear that had just saved his life. Concerned for its well-being, he was relieved when he saw it push itself to its feet. The bear looked over to Arnold and began to walk towards him slowly. Arnold felt as though the pain he was feeling was becoming less and less, and the closer the bear got, the more his fear and anxiety lifted. The bear was calming him, reassuring him. It was a strange sensation, but it felt as though he was healing. Attempting to stand up, he quickly realised he wasn't, however, when his ankle gave way and he fell back to the floor. The bear reached his side, lowering its head. Arnold extended his hand out to touch it and instantly felt the throbbing in his ankle stop. The bear grumbled at Arnold and pushed its giant head against him, further comforting him. The sensation was indescribable, a blend of reality and spectre, a mixed feeling of something being there but not at the same time. The bear sat down, wrapping around Arnold, continuing to soothe his pain. It was waiting for help to come and was going to stay with

Arnold until it arrived, Arnold just knew it. He could feel it. The strange feeling of warmth continued to cover him with rhythmic vibrating waves that pulsated through him. He could have just gone to sleep right then and there, he was that comfortable. He had closed his eyes when he began to hear the calls in the distance.

"Arnold, Arnold, can you hear me?" his dad was shouting as loud as he could, the panic in his voice obvious.

"Over there, Bernard, I can see your spirit beast!" Arnold heard his grandad cry.

The thought of them both being there brought further warmth to Arnold, reassuring him that he was safe.

His dad reached him first, dropping to his knees and propping him up. "Are you okay? Where are you injured?" he demanded in a panic. "I saw you run through the exit with the lions, I thought you were – " he scooped his arms around Arnold and embraced him. Arnold hadn't received a hug like this for a long time and he needed it. Feeling safe for the first time and overwhelmed with emotions, he simply sobbed into his dad's chest.

"Thank you," Bernard said with so much sincerity, it was as if he was talking to his best friend as he reached out and placed his hand on his spirit beast's bowed head. With this, the grizzly bear began to slowly disappear, absorbing back into Bernard's body.

A few moments passed and Arnold's grandad had caught up to the two of them. Lowering his hands to his knees, he stopped to catch his breath, panting as if he could not get enough air in. "He's gone," Elwood said. "He got what he came for. Charles is dead."

# CHAPTER 10

For the next week Arnold felt like he had been wrapped up in cotton wool, as his mum had not let him out of her sight. Although Arnold fully understood this following the attack at the hospital, he was starting to feel suffocated.

"I am going to work now, are you sure you are going to be okay?" Eve asked, hurriedly putting her coat on. "I've made you some soup, it is in the fridge, just warm it up in the pan or the microwave. There is a bread roll in the bread bin."

"I'll be fine, Mum," Arnold sighed. In truth, he was looking forward to a few hours of peace. He hadn't had a moment to himself since he got home from the hospital. His dad had been busy with the Spirit Wardens, following up enquiries about the attack. As much as the initial attack on Charles had been kept away from the media, the attack at the hospital had gained widespread coverage. After all, how often did someone let loose two lion spirit beasts in a hospital?

Arnold's dad had told him that Mr. Whittaker was getting a lot of pressure from the Spirit Wardens to catch the scarred man before anyone else was killed or injured, and the pressure was showing on him. Arnold could also see the toll the situation was taking on his dad. Bernard's face was blotched and his eyes were bloodshot with purple bags forming underneath. He had spent more time at the Athenaeum than he had at home that week, forcing Eve to overcompensate.

"You can't blame me for worrying, Arnold, after everything that has happened to you recently." Eve leaned down to where Arnold was sitting on the sofa and gave him a kiss on top of his head. His plan was to do nothing today. He just wanted to relax and watch TV, his goal to let his mind switch off from everything during some much-needed solitude.

"I'll be home this afternoon, but I will give you a call at lunch time to check in," Eve said.

"Just a text will be fine, Mum," Arnold said, looking back over the sofa as his mum hesitantly left the living room.

When the front door finally shut, the house fell into blissful silence.

Arnold let out an over-the-top sigh of relief. Finally he had some breathing space and could relax on his own without being fussed over.

A sudden rapid knock at the door disrupted Arnold's bliss, and Arnold struggled to his feet, hobbling to the front door, feeling annoyed. Another tap on the door followed as he was making his way to answer.

"Alright," he snapped, "I'm on my way." A pang of frustration got the better of him, his plans for the day already derailed. Pulling the door open, Arnold found Otto standing there, a big grin on his face.

"I want to hear all about it," he said before barging past Arnold and heading straight to the kitchen to fetch himself a drink.

"Come in, Otto," Arnold sighed, his moment of peace and quiet well and truly over.

"This is huge! You fought and survived against a spirit beast attack," Otto started before taking a huge gulp of water and letting out an audible sigh of refreshment. "The whole school is talking about it."

"The whole school?" Arnold hated being the centre of attention and now he dreaded going back to school that little bit more.

"It's not often someone survives an attack like that," Otto continued. "Embrace it. If this doesn't make you popular, nothing will." Otto grinned before walking through to the living room and throwing himself onto the sofa. He picked up the remote and started flicking through the channels.

"Except I didn't fight against the spirit beasts, all I did was run away. It was my dad's bear that fought against them."

"That's just a minor detail, the others at school don't need to know that," Otto said, a beaming smile on his face. "Everyone will want to hear all about it."

"I have already filled you in," Arnold said.

"I've only had a couple of texts from you since last week, its why I came straight round when I knew your mum would be out. My mum said she was going back to work today, so I thought I would take the opportunity to come and see you and get all the gory details." He smiled expectantly at Arnold, waiting for him to open up about the attack.

In truth, Arnold wasn't that keen on re-living the traumatic experience.

"Speaking of which, shouldn't you be at school?" Arnold asked. Otto was dressed in his uniform, his shirt half hanging out of his pants and his tie loose around his neck.

"Free period this morning," he said with a smug smile. "Raine emailed the school and told them I needed to train at the Athenaeum this morning following the attack."

"How did you manage to get her to do that for you?" Arnold was impressed that Otto was already using his newfound membership with the Spirit Wardens to pull strings.

"Just asked her," Otto replied simply, "she seems really nice, and fit." He grinned again.

"She is well out of your league," Arnold laughed.

"Give it a couple of years, once we have finished our training. You'll see." He cast Arnold a cheeky wink to which Arnold simply shook his head.

"It will never happen, Otto."

Tired of trying to find something to watch, Otto tossed the remote control to one side before turning the conversation back on topic. "Anyway, I came over to check in and for you to tell me about everything that happened. What was it like? To be in a spirit battle?"

"I don't really want to talk about it, Otto." Arnold shrugged, rotating his aching shoulder. His arm was cast in a heavy plaster with a sling around his neck.

"Don't be like that," Otto pleaded. "It's me, you tell me everything."

"It was terrifying, Otto," Arnold snapped. What did he expect him to say? That it was exciting? That it was the biggest thrill of his life? "I nearly died. I had to throw myself down multiple flights of stairs as it was the only way to escape. I dread to think what would've happened if my dad hadn't summoned his spirit beast." Arnold could feel a wild frustration building up inside of him. "So forgive me if I don't want to go into detail."

"No need to be like that," Otto said, deflated. He picked himself up from the sofa. "I was just excited to see you, you know." He headed to the doorway to the hall. "I guess I will see you when I see you." And he trudged to the front door.

A wave of guilt washed over Arnold, and he hobbled after his friend. "Otto, wait," he called, but Otto had already left and closed the door behind him. Arnold felt truly awful for how he had snapped at his friend. Taking himself back to the living room, Arnold sat on the sofa and let out a frustrated sigh. His relaxing time to himself was now well and truly ruined, his mood soured. He stared blankly into the TV for a moment as he started to get lost in his thoughts when his phone pinged with a message.

Taking it out of his pocket, he saw he had a text from Everett. His heart skipped a beat as he opened it up to read it.

*Hey Arnold, hope you are feeling better. George has spoke with her granny and she has said to swing by her shop after school, we will meet you there. Think she has a tonic she wants to give you to help you heal up, ready for school. Speak later, Everett xx*

Arnold read the message twice but focused for a moment on the kisses that Everett had put at the end of the message. He instantly found that his spirits had lifted. He just needed to wait out the rest of the school day now. He quickly texted back, rewriting the message multiple times before settling on:

*See you there*

He followed this up with a quick text to Otto.

*Sorry, it's just too soon to talk about the attack. Meet me at George's granny's shop after school. Apparently she wants to see me.*

Putting his phone in his pocket, Arnold sat back and started watching TV. He was looking forward to getting out later but for now, he simply just wanted to let his brain switch off.

~

As soon as it hit three o'clock, Arnold set off at a steady hobble down to Union Road, the main street that ran through the centre of Oswaldtwistle. George's granny's shop sat just opposite the mini supermarket. He had passed it hundreds of times but never actually been inside.

It was a curious little shop that, from outside, looked in need of some renovations, but by all accounts, it had remained popular enough to stay open. A worn, brown sign hung across the top of the glass storefront, the gilded letters so faded that

Arnold could not make out what the shop was actually called. A small sign stood on the pavement outside of the front door that simply said, 'open', written in chalk.

The glass door felt light as Arnold pushed it open, a bell above his head giving a light ring as he made his way inside. He surveyed the shop and was taken aback at how chaotic and untidy it was. Piles and piles of books were stacked on a large table to his immediate right, no order to them apparent. Some books lay open, some on their backs, some stood upright. The walls were littered with all manner of strange devices that Arnold had never seen before. He didn't know if they were weapons or artefacts. A strange, thick smoke hung in the air which felt suffocating enough that Arnold had to cough. The floral smell was overpowering, almost like lavender.

"Hello?" he called uncertainly, but there was no answer. He called once more, this time a little more forceful.

"Coming, dear," a croaked voice called, followed by a jingling sound. Rows and rows of braids hung down loosely in a doorway behind the counter. Two spindly hands separated them before George's granny stepped out from behind them. It was clear to Arnold the second he saw her where George got her quirky dress sense from.

The elderly woman wasn't the tallest of people, her dark grey hair tied up into a bun on her head. All manner of beads and trinkets were fastened into her rolls of hair, making it look like a bird's nest. On the end of her nose, she wore a pair of spectacles that enlarged her eyes to a gargantuan size, which caused Arnold to wonder just how bad her vision was.

"Yes, dear?" she asked through blinking eyes.

Arnold looked around the shop nervously. There was no sign of George or Everett. "George said for me to come here, she said you had a tonic for me."

The woman stepped towards him to get a better look through squinting eyes, then gave Arnold a warming smile that relaxed him. "You must be Arnold," she said. "Come, come over here."

She wandered past Arnold towards another cluttered table, on the centre of which sat a small cauldron. Twigs, leaves, berries, and all manner of ingredients lay scattered on either side of it.

"It's nearly ready." She smiled as she stepped up onto a small stool and leaned over the top of the cauldron to take in a deep sniff, lapping her tongue against the roof of her mouth as if she were tasting it. "Something isn't quite right though." Her wrinkled brow furrowed in deep thought. She seemed to ponder for a moment before saying, "Turmeric." She hopped down from the little stool and headed to the other side of the shop where rows and rows of jars sat on rickety wooden shelves. She looked over them for a moment before pointing upwards. "Be a dear and grab that for me."

Arnold obliged, grabbing the dusty jar and passing it to George's granny.

"Pass me those vanilla pods, too," she said, waving her finger at the other side of the shelves. "Oh, and the horua root," she added, waving towards the centre of the shelves. Arnold took them down one by one and handed them over. George's granny held these in her arms before placing them on the table and hopping back up behind the cauldron. She shook the turmeric, allowing plentiful to dust into the cauldron before adding a vanilla pod. She then snapped the dry horua root and dropped it in with a light splash.

After she gave the mixture a stir, she took in another deep inhale before saying, "That's better. It doesn't taste the best, but I find the horua root and the vanilla will take that edge off. Hopefully it will lessen the nausea, too."

Arnold couldn't help but worry just what on earth she had made for him.

"It still needs a little time to brew, not too long, mind you, about five or ten minutes."

Arnold stood awkwardly, not knowing how to pass conversation. Tapping his hands lightly on his thighs, the only thing audible was the bubbling concoction and the ticking of a clock somewhere out of sight.

"I believe you're the boy who has been accepted into the Spirit Warden's, aren't you? Georgina has been telling me all about it, yes, very curious." She paused in an almost trance-like state. "Very curious, indeed. Be careful, boy. Those Spirit Wardens are not all they're cracked up to be." She studied Arnold closely, her large eyes scanning over him. "I would have thought Elwood would have warned you about them by now, especially after everything that happened." She tilted her head slightly, a slight spark of remembrance igniting in her eyes. "You have your grandma's eyes."

In an instant, Arnold's wavering attention snapped back. "My – my grandma?" he stammered, taken aback. "Did you know her?"

"Of course," she said, nodding with a smile.

Arnold had so many questions but no idea where to start as his mind raced with this new information. Perhaps he at last would find out about his grandma what his family had kept from him all these years.

The sound of the bell disrupted their conversation, and both turned to look at the door into the shop.

"Ah, Georgina, dear, you are here. We have a lot to get on with this evening."

"Granny, it's George," George sighed, albeit with a smile.

"Nonsense, I will call you by the name your parents gifted you."

"Granny, my dads are happy with me shortening it, you know this, we have had this conversation one hundred times over." George came bustling in and wrapped her arms around her granny, who in turn placed her delicate arms around her granddaughter before patting her lightly on the back. It was an endearing moment which helped Arnold capture just how close the two of them were.

Everett followed George into the shop and gave Arnold a big smile. To Arnold's surprise, Everett stepped forward and gave him a hug.

"Ouch," Arnold said, wincing at Everett's strength.

"Sorry," she said, stepping away from him. "I'm just glad you're okay."

"I think he is getting injured on purpose just to get all these hugs from you," came Otto's teasing voice as he trailed into the shop. Arnold hadn't noticed the bell ringing as he walked in, he'd been so engrossed in Everett's unexpected embrace.

Arnold gave Otto a death stare to which Otto simply shrugged as he started rummaging through the books that were littered on the table in front of him.

"How do you find anything in here?" he asked abruptly.

"It's organised mess," George laughed. "I must admit I used to struggle with it, but I guarantee if you ask my granny for anything, she will know exactly where it is." She stepped away from her granny and gave Arnold a more delicate hug than Everett had. "I'm so glad you're okay, we were so worried when we heard about the attack. I was telling Granny that you had broken your arm and damaged your ligaments in your ankle when she told me to get you to come here for a remedy." George scurried behind the table and peered into the small, bubbling cauldron. She sniffed it before beaming in delight. "It smells ready, Granny." She sniffed again and paused for a moment. "Is that aniseed?" she asked.

Her granny gave a warm smile, "It is, dear. We will make a spirit-weaver out of you yet," she said as she stepped behind the cauldron to give it a stir. "Georgina, can you fetch me a flask from over there?"

George went and gathered a flask before passing it to her granny, who gathered up the remedy in a large pipette before adding it to the flask, her trembling hands filling Arnold with dread that she was more likely to empty it all over the floor. Arnold and the others continued to watch on in awe at George's granny's precision as she filled the flask.

She finally put down the pipette and passed the flask to Arnold, along with a lid. "Here you go," she said, still smiling. "No doubt you are still in pain from your broken arm. This will help it heal and make it less painful for you while your bones fuse back together."

"Thanks," Arnold said politely. The flask was warm to touch, and when he sniffed the top of it, he could smell the aniseed that George had mentioned. It was extremely strong and burned the back of his nose, causing him to cough. If he was honest, it wasn't the nicest of smells and he was definitely in two minds about whether he was even going to drink it now. However, he didn't want to offend George's granny given that she had made it especially for him.

Her granny watched Arnold in anticipation with her magnified eyes. "Well, go on," she said, "drink it."

Arnold shuddered at the thought, but reluctantly brought it up to his lips and took a large gulp. It tasted foul, the aniseed burning the back of his throat as well as the piping hot water. Arnold spluttered, choking back the urge to vomit it back up.

George's granny chuckled and clapped her hands together in glee. "It's definitely brewed right, makes everyone cough and splutter but don't worry, it will have your bones good as new in no time. The key is to sip it, not gulp it down, that's a common mistake."

The others sniggered too before Arnold offered it to Otto. "You want to try some?"

Otto shook his head, looking repulsed. "You're okay, thanks."

"Thank you so much," Arnold said, "you really didn't have to." Deep down he wished she really hadn't but now he felt obligated to drink it, and if it helped him get back to training at the Athenaeum even sooner, that was a bonus. After all, he had been injured before he had even had the chance to start his real training.

"You are more than welcome. Say hi to Elwood for me. Tell him to pop over for a brew sometime."

"I will do," Arnold said, smiling. He desperately wanted to ask about his grandma but did not feel it appropriate to simply spring it on her, especially in front of all of his friends.

"Now, Georgina, we have lots to get through tonight." She turned to George who was busy tidying up the ingredients around the cauldron and putting them back into their respective jars.

"I guess we will see you later," Everett laughed and the three of them made their way out of the shop.

Otto let out a sigh and gasped for air as soon as the door shut behind him, acting like he had been starved of oxygen for the five minutes he had been inside. "That was unbearable, I feel like the incense has stuck to my skin!" He started patting himself down like he was on fire before smelling his arms.

Everett and Arnold let out a laugh in tandem with one another.

"Well, I best get going," Everett said. "I was thinking, maybe I could swing by and help you with your homework for the next week or so until you are back in school."

"That sounds great," Arnold responded, a little over eager in his reply.

"No worries, I will swing by after school tomorrow and we will take it from there." She gave them both a wave and set off.

Arnold found himself staring in disbelief that Everett was going to be coming around to his house to help him with his homework. His jaw dropped slightly.

"Ah, love's young dream," Otto teased, earning himself an elbow to the ribs. "Ow!"

Arnold laughed. For the first time in a while his spirits were lifted. Even though he still had plenty of questions unanswered about his grandma, the scarred man, and his spirit beast, for now his friends had managed to distract his mind, even if only for a brief moment. He took another look at the remedy before taking a sip this time, then set off back home.

## CHAPTER 11

It was another two weeks before Arnold returned to school, and a few more before he began to feel recovered from his meeting with the scarred man and the lions of the Aether. Between school and spending his evenings in the Athenaeum, there was not much else that Arnold was able to do other than read, given that his arm was out of commission.

Everett remained true to her word and had been coming around to help Arnold complete his homework, given that he couldn't write.

Arnold hated having his arm in a cast, not just because of the limitations this put on him but also because of the insanity-inducing itch he would often experience halfway down his arm that he was unable to rid himself of. He had, however, enjoyed Everett's ongoing company, the two of them getting along better than ever. Arnold was pleased to learn that they seemed to have a lot in common.

Evenings at the Athenaeum had been slow, with Arnold spending his time trying to find out more on the lions of the Aether and the Blade of the Spirits, but so far, he only had the one book that he had found by Betsy Devon to go off. He had now read the book from front to back twice over. In the latter pages of the chapter around the Blade of the Spirits, the book had also confirmed the story that his dad had told him and Otto the night of the attack. The rest of the book had just listed different expeditions that Betsy and her team had been on attempting to uncover varying artefacts from around the world. In truth, Arnold wasn't much interested in the other expeditions, only wanting to know more about the Blade of the Spirits.

Arnold's readings and research had gotten him no closer to finding out more about the blade, the lions, or the scarred man and what linked them to Charles.

Arnold had not attended Charles's funeral. After all, he didn't know Charles beyond the chance encounter on his birthday. His dad and grandad had attended though, with his grandad taking his friend's death particularly hard. Arnold hadn't seen his grandad much over the last few weeks. Even when he would call around for a cup of tea and check in on Arnold's recovery, Arnold hadn't been able to get him alone to talk to him about Charles and how the two of them knew each other. When Arnold had tried once or twice to broach the topic with him, his grandad would quickly change the subject.

Now that Arnold was feeling back to normal, he planned to call around one evening after school to catch up with him and try again at getting more information, but it was like trying to crack the hardest of safes. His grandad's stubbornness was certainly a trait Arnold had picked up and he was not going to give up until he found out more.

More frustrating than anything, Arnold hadn't had any more dreams about flying since the attack. He craved the thrill of flying so badly and would do anything to experience this again. Despite this, Arnold had been looking forward to today, specifically eleven twenty am. He had been crossing off the days on his calendar in anticipation.

Today was the day that he finally got to have his cast taken off, and after a restless morning at school, Arnold found himself sat in the consultant's room at the hospital with the doctor using the large sheers to cut off the plaster cast. The relief Arnold felt once it was removed was fantastic, and he instantly started itching the spot on the inside of his arm that had been driving ham mad for the last six weeks.

"Now, your cast is off, but you still need to rest it for a couple of weeks." The doctor spoke in a patronising manner, as though Arnold was about to start doing handstands and cartwheels as soon as he left the room. "Try not to do anything too strenuous. It might ache a bit now the cast is off, but it is nothing that some paracetamol will not fix."

The doctor got Arnold to move his arm around in multiple positions and rotations before deciding he was happy with his movement and discharging him. Arnold exited the hospital with his dad and made the short walk back to the car, rotating his shoulder and trying to get used to having free movement again. His arm felt so much lighter now which was a strange sensation.

Climbing into the car, Arnold sighed at the prospect of having to go back to school. He picked his bag up from the footwell and took out his planner to see what his afternoon sessions were. Geography and Cooking.

Bernard started the car up, ready to drop Arnold off and head back to work. "It was a bit traumatic, that," he said as he reversed out of the parking bay.

Arnold felt that the removal of the cast had been the most un-traumatic thing to happen to him in the past few weeks. It was nothing compared to his birthday, the Bloodbound Ritual, or throwing himself down two flights of stairs while trying to outrun the lions of the Aether.

Bernard grinned. "Think you need to take the rest of the day off, son. Let's call it a well-being day." He winked at Arnold as the two smiled at each other.

Relief washed over Arnold. He could finish the afternoon relaxing at home playing on his Xbox.

*Or I could go and see grandad,* he thought.

At home, Arnold quickly went inside and got changed from his school uniform. After throwing on some jeans and his blue football shirt from his favourite team, Everton F.C., he made himself a quick sandwich, then headed out to make his way to his grandad's house. He thought he might ring to let him know he was on his way over, then decided against this given that his grandad very rarely answered his phone.

It was a lovely day, and the sun was uncharacteristically casting large shadows from the buildings and trees around Arnold as he walked to his grandad's. It was a nice feeling as the sun warmed Arnold's face and arms, bringing back memories of the strange sensation he experienced when his dad's spirit beast had sat around him to comfort him.

Arnold knocked on the brown, wooden door of Elwood's home, a semi-detached house that sat at the bottom of a pristinely kept cul-de-sac.

As he stood waiting for his grandad to answer, he could feel the heat of the sun on the back of his head, which still felt soothing against his skin. When there was no answer, Arnold knocked again, this time slightly harder just in case his grandad hadn't heard him. There was no answer again, so Arnold decided to try the front door, thinking that if it was locked, he may have gone out for something.

Arnold tried the door handle and pushed against the door, which creaked slowly open. A spark of worry erupted in his chest, but as Arnold stepped inside and moved into the hallway, he realised that his grandad was fast asleep in his armchair, the low grumbling noise coming from his nose showing he was in a deep sleep.

Something caught his eye immediately: upstairs, a loft hatch was open with a set of steps leading up to it. Arnold hadn't even known his grandad had a loft. Intrigued as to what his grandad had been doing up there, Arnold had an overwhelming urge to find out what was up there.

*It won't cause any harm to have a look*, he thought.

Arnold began to sneak up the stairs, trying his hardest not to disturb his grandad, the stairs creaking ever so slightly as he made his way towards the top. Halfway up, Elwood stirred, causing Arnold to freeze in his tracks. After a few moments of shuffling around, Elwood began snoring again, and Arnold set off to the top of the stairs once more.

Arnold reached the bottom of the ladder, more curious than ever at what might be in the loft. All he now had to do was climb the steps without disturbing his grandad. He took a deep breath and pulled himself onto the rungs, finding them sturdier than he expected. He climbed up into the loft space, pushing up from his knees to a standing position.

The room was dark, and there was a damp musk in the air that left a bitter taste in Arnold's mouth. He found the pull chord switch and tugged on it lightly, then waited for a second as the light above him began to flicker before switching on.

"Wow," Arnold breathed. The room had clearly not been in frequent use given the thick layer of dust that sat on top of everything, but it looked as though the contents of the attic belonged in a museum. There were glass cases on either side of the room with varying objects on display, from vases to pieces of armour. Arnold surveyed the room while taking in all the varying objects. His eyes were drawn to footprints on the dusty floor that led to the corner of the room. Guessing this was where his grandad must have been, Arnold followed the tracks.

In the corner of the room sat an old wooden trunk, the rusted metal frame around the edges barely visible through the dirt that had collected on top of it over the years. There was a padlock on the trunk but on closer inspection, Arnold found the key was still inside. Intrigued, Arnold turned the key until the padlock clicked and cracked open. The hinges creaked as he opened the chest slowly, still not wanting to disturb his grandad. Arnold's shadow obscured the contents of the trunk, so he positioned himself to allow some light past. That's when he noticed what looked like an old photograph. Arnold picked this up to examine it closer. A section had been torn off, but he could clearly make out his much younger-looking grandad standing beside two other people Arnold didn't recognise. Arnold knew his grandad liked visiting countries all over the world, and judging by his clothing in the picture, this picture had been taken on one of his many expeditions. The trio appeared to be standing in a forest in front of a giant tree.

Arnold placed the torn photo to his side and saw that there was a long item wrapped in a red cloth. He reached in, eager to see what it was, and found that it was quite heavy. Leaning into the trunk with both hands, he removed the weighted object before turning and placing it on the dust-laden floor. Curious, Arnold began to unfold the cloth, feeling a strange pull to the item that he couldn't quite put his finger on. After removing the cloth, he stared at the item, not knowing what exactly it was.

To Arnold, it looked like a weapon – and a really old one at that. It resembled a cricket bat, except that both sides were flat and etched with intricate carvings that Arnold recognised as hieroglyphs. On each side appeared to be animal totems etched into the dark stained wood, however Arnold was unable to make out what these were. The hilt was bound with a thick maroon thread, that was coarse to the touch. At the bottom of the hilt, more intricate carvings of what Arnold assumed was a spirit beast had been etched, although he could not tell what it was. Around the outer edge of the paddle-like object was finely polished black stone, which had been inserted into the wood all the way around, making it look almost like a chainsaw. This was the strangest looking thing that Arnold had ever seen, and he was bemused as to what it actually was and what it was doing in his grandad's attic.

*Pick it up.* The urge was too great to ignore.

The pull to the blade felt stronger than ever, and as Arnold grasped the hilt, a surge of energy ran through his arm which startled him into letting it go. The strange item dropped to the floor with a dull thud.

Arnold stopped for a moment, thinking that something felt strange, different from before. It only took a moment for him to realise that the background noise of his grandad's snoring had stopped. Arnold spun around to find Elwood's face poking through the loft hatch, frowning at him. Arnold had been that engrossed in the object, he hadn't heard his grandad coming up the stairs or the ladder.

"Thought you were a bloody burglar," Elwood scoffed. "Why on earth are you not at school and why are you up here?"

"I had my cast taken off and Dad said I didn't have to go back to school so I thought I would call here. You were asleep and the loft was open, so I wanted to have a look." Arnold's eyes were drawn back to the object on the floor.

Elwood followed his gaze and let out a sigh. "Suppose you want to know what it is? It's called a macuahuitl."

"A mac-what?"

"Mac-ua-hu-itl," Elwood repeated more slowly. "It's a very old weapon. I stumbled across it years ago when I was a young Doyen. I kept it, even used it a couple of times in combat. It's stronger than it looks, you know. Took it everywhere with me once I had found it."

Arnold was aghast at what his grandad had just said. "Combat?" His grandad never spoke much about when he was a Doyen.

"Yes, combat. Happens sometimes when you're a Doyen. Back then anyway. Not so much now, though, thank goodness."

Arnold didn't know what to say. He couldn't imagine his grandad in combat, let alone swinging this macuahuitl around. Elwood had never really discussed his Doyen days with Arnold, and he didn't want to miss this opportunity.

"It's the most bizarre weapon I have ever seen," Arnold replied. He wanted to know more about the strange relic that lay on the floor in front of them. He continued to feel drawn to the weapon as though he was magnetised to it, unable to take his eyes off it.

"That sword has got me out of some serious trouble," Elwood continued. "The wood has no blemishes on it despite being used because of the ancient way the wood was treated. Or at least, that's my theory. I never found any solid evidence of this." He chuckled like he had an in joke with himself that only a few people would understand. "The sharpened stone that is inserted around the outer edge of the sword is called obsidian. It is highly polished and treated the right way to enable this sword to be just as lethal as any sword cast of iron or steel. When used properly, anyway."

Arnold didn't know what to think. His grandad never spoke about his past days as a Doyen, but here he was, suddenly more animated and keener to discuss than ever before.

"Why is all this stuff up here, Grandad?" Arnold stepped towards a glass case that had an old vase sat inside it. It looked basic, with no etchings or intricate carvings on it, however it looked old. Really old. "I thought the Spirit Wardens would want all of these?" He rubbed his hand on the glass to brush away some of the dust.

"As I progressed in the Spirit Wardens, I came to realise that they didn't need to know about everything." Elwood picked up the macuahuitl, re-wrapped it in the cloth, then placed it back inside the chest. "I used to enjoy collecting things. There used to be a purpose, but in the end, well, it just ended up staying in here. There is stuff up here that the Spirit Wardens have no idea about. We found relics and artefacts from all over the world, your grandma and I." He suddenly stopped, as if surprised at himself for acknowledging his wife.

Arnold had no idea what she looked like given that his grandad had no photos in the house of her. His dad had always told him that the memories of her were simply too painful. Bernard himself knew little of his own mum, and had learned not to ask questions, knowing how much it hurt Elwood to talk about her. As a result, Arnold's grandma had faded away into history as though she never existed. Arnold always respected this for his grandad's sake, but now he had a burning desire to find out more about her.

Sensing the opportunity, he seized the moment to ask something he had never dared to ask before. "What happened to her, Grandad?" There was a delicateness to Arnold's voice, not wanting to upset him but also yearning to know more about his grandma.

"Forty years." His grandad let out a defeated sigh, as if the two words he had just spoken had took a tremendous weight off his shoulders. "It has been forty years since I last saw her." He closed the trunk where he had just placed the macuahuitl and sat himself on top, exhaling with trembling breath.

Arnold could not believe it; his grandad was opening up to him about his grandma, something that he had never done with Bernard as far as Arnold knew. Eager to listen, Arnold dragged a footstool closer to the centre of the room before wiping off the dust, leaving a small plume of dirt floating around in the air. He could taste this slightly as he sat and took in a deep breath in anticipation of what his grandad was about to tell him.

"We were in Africa at the time, a few of us. It was part holiday and part exploration, that's what we liked to do back then. Well, what we needed to do. Your dad was actually with us. It was the first time we had been away since the day that he was born." A smile etched across Elwood's face, as if remembering becoming a parent for the first time. "Your grandma and I had always wanted to visit Africa, so when a few of our friends invited us over to see them, we decided that we would join. They had been working over there for the last year."

"Charles?"

"Yes, Charles and his wife." Elwood's voice had stopped trembling and the words came out of his mouth more smoothly now, not forced. "Bernard was two years old and a right handful. Just like you used to be." He chuckled again. "Bernard could walk and was beginning to start forming words for the first time. Everything he saw, he wanted, and you needed to keep an eye on him because he was as quick as a flash."

Arnold sat frozen on the footstool, transfixed by the story that he was being told.

"Charles's wife wanted to go visit an old temple, so we decided to tag along for the experience, hoping to learn more about the local culture. That's when everything went wrong." Elwood began to look pained again, and his voice began to tremble. "Your grandma, she was the most beautiful woman I had ever seen, and the only thing that matched her beauty was the fierceness with which she would protect her family."

Arnold's grandad was struggling to talk about her now and for a moment, Arnold considered stopping him, seeing the pain he was going through.

Elwood exhaled and continued. "She was a dragon, Arnold, well at least, her spirit beast was."

Arnold nearly fell from the footstool. Dragon spirit beasts were somewhat of an unknown quantity, having been so rare throughout history. One thing that was known by historians was the fiery rage that the bearers of this spirit beast possessed.

"She was an amazing person, Arnold. She was kind and

loving and caring and just wanted to do right by everyone." His voice was sharp and direct as if he were defending her.

Confused, Arnold continued to listen to his grandad's words in silence, afraid to interrupt.

"As you know, the dragon spirit beast is the rarest form of spirit beast. No one has ever known anyone to have one, not in recent generations, anyway. That is, apart from me and your grandma. Your grandma kept this hidden from everyone, even her own family."

Arnold could feel a lump forming in his throat. He was learning about a woman that if not for her, he wouldn't exist. "Why?" he asked, not understanding fully what his grandad was alluding to. "Why would she not tell anyone?"

"Because she would have been taken away, experimented on like some lab rat by the Spirit Wardens. They would want to know the source of her power." There was anger in his voice now. "Dragon spirit beasts are feared. Some people may have even tried to kill her because of it, because of the power it possessed, the power your grandma possessed. So, your grandma kept it hidden inside her, never used it, never needed to until the day that we lost her. Our research had led us to believe that the blade we were looking for had the ability to trap her spirit beast inside. She would have become a menial, but she would have been safe, and it is what your grandma wanted. All I can say is that we found the blade. We had it in our hands, and that is when her spirit beast took over. It did not wish to be trapped, and so it consumed her."

"Consumed?"

"Yes, it took control of her mind, her body. Just like that, she was gone forever. In her place was this vile spirit beast that only knew of anger and fury. It attacked us, desperate to escape, and we had no option but to defend ourselves."

Arnold stood up, was upset about his grandma but also confused as to why he was suddenly being told all of this. "Why now? Why are you talking to me about her?" Arnold could feel the warmth of the tears that were rolling down his cheeks. He felt completely overwhelmed by the situation. He continued to focus on his grandad, who looked more vulnerable than Arnold had ever seen him.

"Because I'm scared, Arnold, I'm absolutely petrified."

"What of?"

"You."

Arnold sat back down, confused by his grandad's words. Why would his grandad be scared of him? Arnold would never hurt his grandad in a million years, he was the most important person in the world to him.

Elwood wiped away the tears from his cheek and sniffed, his face becoming blotchy. "Your dreams, Arnold, it's your dreams." He gathered himself before continuing. "Your grandma used to tell me about these vivid dreams of flying that she used to have when she was younger, even speaking of a tower that kept recurring in her dream. Your dad told me all about your Bloodbound Ritual and your split aura. You showed the sign of the dragon, you're having the same dreams that your grandma had."

The realisation dawned on Arnold. There had been that much that had happened recently, he had not been looking into the identity of his spirit beast. He had solely been focused on the Blade of the Spirits, the scarred man, and the lions of the Aether. "You think I have a dragon spirit beast, don't you?"

"Yes, Arnold, and it absolutely fills me with dread."

"Why? What is so bad about it? It might be rare, but I am sure I could handle it," Arnold insisted, a slight cockiness coming over him with the realisation that he may have the rarest of spirit beasts inside of him.

Elwood stood up and walked across the room to the glass cabinet where the bowl Arnold had looked at earlier was placed. Arnold spun on the footstool and faced the back of his grandad, only able to see part of his face in the reflection in the glass panel.

"Your grandma was the nicest, kindest person that I have ever come across. She was simply beautiful inside and out. That – that thing still consumed her to protect itself. She had no control over it." His voice became slightly raised, and there was no mistaking the anger he felt around this. "It took her away from us, and I think that it lies within you too, Arnold. That is what scares me more than anything on this earth. The thought of it consuming you, too. You know what happens if you are consumed? You lose all control. The beast takes over as if you were a puppet unable to ever escape. The Spirit Wardens know that you may have a dragon spirit beast, and that means they are watching you, closer than you could imagine. I won't let them take you away."

Arnold didn't know what to say to his grandad. He felt there was more to what his grandad was telling him, but didn't feel that he could take any more information in. He truly felt at saturation point, a sponge that was holding as much water as possible and he did not want to start leaking out what he had just been told. Arnold stood up and walked over to his grandad and gave him the tightest hug he could muster. Elwood placed his arms around Arnold and squeezed him back, and Arnold felt comforted as if wrapped in a warm blanket. He knew his grandad would protect him from anything. He always had, since he was little. He felt safe when his grandad was with him, and he wanted his grandad to feel the same around him, now that he was older. He wanted him to know that he was going to be okay, everything was going to be okay.

Arnold knew that his grandad's concerns must be severe for him to talk to him about his grandma, but for now, he had no more questions. For now, in this moment, he simply wanted to comfort his grandad, to help him offload the unbearable weight he had been keeping to himself for so many years. The two cried together, taking comfort from one another.

But the nagging through re-surfaced in the back of Arnold's mind.

*What if I could control it?*

# CHAPTER 12

Arnold was back at home and feeling in a state of shock from what he had just learned from his grandad. His grandma had a dragon spirit beast, the rarest, most dangerous form a spirit beast could take, and Elwood was worried that Arnold too had this spirit beast inside of him. The conversation had answered some of the deep, burning questions Arnold had from the night he heard his dad and grandad arguing, and he understood why his grandad had been against him beginning training. It was because of the risk associated with having a dragon spirit beast that had destroyed his grandma, and he didn't want it to destroy him, too.

Elwood's fears were that if he was indeed like his grandma and had a dragon spirit beast, he would have to learn to hide it like she had done, learn to suppress it so that the power of it did not take over. History could not repeat itself.

Arnold lay on his bed staring up at the ceiling, his thoughts again whirling around his head. He was beginning to get answers but did not like the way they were going. He had been obsessed around having his spirit beast for as long as he could remember, cursing his luck at not developing like his friends were, not becoming in tune with his auro the same as the others.

Now there was a high chance that his spirit beast could be a dragon, which meant that he would have to learn to hide it and not use it. He'd be unable to become a Doyen, and he would have to pretend to be a menial, to act as though he had no spirit beast connected to him at all.

Feeling his frustration building inside, he began to wonder if this was why he had a bit of a temper and experienced fits of jealousy for his friends like he had been doing recently. At least that would make sense, he told himself, trying to justify the strong whirlwind of emotions he had been experiencing lately.

His dad must have already known about his grandma and had a different way of wanting to protect him. It was clear to Arnold that this was what had caused the argument between him and Elwood a couple of months ago. However, Bernard must have been prepared for Arnold to know, as he had given his blessing for Arnold to speak with his grandad about it prior to the attack at the hospital.

Arnold looked at his watch, realising that school had finished and before too long he would need head to the Spirit Wardens and meet up with Otto. His grandad had warned him not to discuss the dragon with anyone, but Otto was next to him at the Bloodbound Ritual and had witnessed the dragon symbol that had illuminated above Arnold during the initiation. He felt as though his head was going to explode due to the amount of information he was trying to process. At least Otto could try and help him pick things apart or even help him do a bit more research.

There was a knock at the front door, soft enough for Arnold to know that it wasn't Otto but distinct enough to recognise who it was. Arnold had become accustomed to the firm knock from Everett's visits while he had his cast on, and a smile fell on his face as his mood lifted with Everett calling around. Arnold skipped down the stairs but slowed his pace as he arrived at the front door, trying his hardest to play it cool as he opened the front door.

He opened the door and there was Everett, her warm smile instantly lifting him. The sun caught her perfectly soft, dark skin, ensuring that her bright blue eyes shone brighter than he had ever seen them, like sapphires cast in ice.

"Come in." He pulled the door further back and stepped to the side, allowing her to enter the house.

She smiled and stepped through the front door. "I just wanted to see how the big day had gone. How's it feeling?"

So much had happened today that for a moment, Arnold had no clue what Everett was talking about. The fact that he'd had his cast removed felt like a distant memory. He rotated his shoulder and felt his arm ache slightly. He hadn't even noticed the dull pain all afternoon, his mind had been that busy, but suddenly it felt like it was catching up with him now that he had been reminded of it. It began to throb quite heavily, and as a sense of nausea overcame him, Arnold tried to play it cool.

"It's fine. Doctor said I have to take it easy for a while, but I'll be back to my best soon."

"Won't need me to come around to help with your homework anymore then, will you?" There was a playfulness in Everett's voice, and Arnold was startled to realise that she was flirting with him.

Arnold began to stutter, wishing for a moment that Otto was there to speak on his behalf, but he needed to learn to keep calm in these situations like Otto would. He needed to channel his inner Otto.

"You can still come round," he said hurriedly. He couldn't have sounded any less like Otto. "We can do our homework together." He paused, not feeling confident of Everett's response as she didn't reply instantaneously. "That's, if you want to."

"Do you want me to?" she replied in a playful manner again.

Sensing that Everett was fishing for answers, Arnold felt his confidence grow. "Yeah, I do." He smiled at her, realising that she actually looked just as nervous as him. "Everett, I just wanted to say, thanks for helping me."

"You don't need to thank me."

"But I want to. I would be behind on a lot of my work if you hadn't helped me."

"It would have been cruel, to leave Otto to help you do your work." She laughed. "No one deserves that."

"True."

"I just wanted to pop by and see how your arm was with the cast off, so I guess I best get going."

"Wait there, just for a moment." Arnold shot up the stairs and returned quickly with a box of chocolates in his hand. "Erm, I got these for you, you know, to say thanks."

"Sweet." Everett smiled at Arnold appreciatively. "Surprised you came up with that yourself."

Arnold smirked.

"You didn't, did you?"

"That would be telling." Arnold knew full well it was his grandad's idea.

Everett stepped forward and placed a gentle kiss on Arnold's cheek, and his face immediately began to blush. Everett stood back and smiled at Arnold again and suddenly he felt like he had all the confidence in the world, like he could achieve anything today.

"See you at school tomorrow." She smiled again and headed off, leaving Arnold stood there with a goofy smile.

He was experiencing actual happiness, something that had been missing from his life for a while now.

Arnold felt on top of the world.

When he arrived at the Atheneum later, Raine greeted him

with a smile as he made his way to the library. He felt like he had a stride in his step, a swagger he had never had before. He liked this feeling.

Arriving at the library, he placed his finger on the pressure pad and the glass double doors unfrosted before opening. Inside, he found Otto pressing the screen on the table in the centre of the Athenaeum, determined as ever to get into it.

"You're never going to get in," Arnold called out.

Otto stopped what he was doing and turned to face him. "What's happened to you? You look different," he said suspiciously, as if he noticed that Arnold had an unfamiliar air about him.

"Everett kissed me," Arnold said, a smug grin on his face.

"Seriously? She kissed you?" Otto responded in disbelief, practically shouting the words.

"Yup. And my cast is off."

"Sounds like a belting day, that." Otto winked, the best way he could show his pride in Arnold receiving his first kiss from a girl.

"That's not the half of it, there's so much more that I need to tell you." Arnold proceeded to tell Otto about his grandad's loft space, the macuahuitl, his grandma, and her dragon spirit beast.

"That's a lot to take in, mate," Otto said afterwards. "So, your grandad thinks that your spirit beast is a dragon?" His face lit up like a Christmas tree. "That's pretty epic, to be fair." Otto looked excited by the prospect of Arnold's spirit beast. "Kaden would never mess with you again."

"I think my grandad was worried about me losing my temper. It sounded like that was what he was trying to tell me happened to my grandma."

"Need to keep a lid on it then, mate. Was there not a book up there about dragon spirit beasts? Maybe we can start there. Try and get some more information, that will help us." Otto pointed over to the wall of books on the far side of the Athenaeum indicating where he thought the book might be. "We have the ladders, remember? We will use them."

"I am sure I took it home with me," Arnold said, desperately trying to remember. He was sure he had placed it in his bag alongside the journal of Betsy Devon, which meant the book would be at home.

The glass double doors at the entrance unfrosted and opened, and Mr. Whittaker walked into the room. He did not look happy, but it was no different from what they had become accustomed to.

Mr. Whittaker was wearing a nice, light grey suit with a white shirt and pink tie. He stood within the Athenaeum and began to straighten his cuffs as he spoke. "Please can you both come this way." He spun on his highly polished shoes and set off to exit the Athenaeum.

Looking at each other and gesturing for the other to go first, Otto decided to take the lead on this occasion and set off to follow Mr. Whittaker with Arnold just behind him.

Mr. Whittaker led them back into the main reception area for the Spirit Wardens and spun back on his heels again, giving them both little time to adjust their speed and avoid clattering into him.

"How is your research?" There was a coldness to his voice that Arnold had not noticed the night of the Bloodbound Ritual. In fact, ever since their initiation, Mr. Whittaker had made them feel as though it were an inconvenience for them to even be there, even though it was him that insisted on them both joining.

"You have had two months so far which seems to be a lot longer than usual for most candidates. I would like an update."

Arnold didn't like how he seemed to talk at them and not to them.

Otto stepped forward and raised his hand as if saluting Mr.

Whittaker in a sarcastic manner. "Sir, my spirit beast is definitely from the big cat family."

Mr. Whittaker looked less than impressed with Otto's salute and stared at him until Otto lowered his arm. "Two months to find that out? I could have told you that just from your auro totem in the Bloodbound Ritual," he scolded. "Please tell me you have more than that, Master Redburn?"

"Well, with me becoming more athletic and stronger as well as showing characteristics such as loyalty, you know, with still being friends with Arnold despite him not being able to keep up with me."

Arnold tried not to wince, feeling this wouldn't end well. As usual, Otto had mistaken cockiness for confidence.

"That would leave me with options such as the panther, the leopard, or the jaguar," Otto continued, oblivious. "If I had to hazard a guess, sir." Otto saluted Mr. Whittaker again as he signed off on his monologue. He looked across at Raine who was typing away at her desk and winked at her. She smirked back at Otto.

Arnold fought the urge to roll his eyes. When Otto felt he had a crowd to play to was usually when he got himself into trouble.

"Address me in such a patronising manner again, and I will have you thrown out of the Spirit Wardens, Master Redburn," Mr. Whittaker said calmly. "Two months that has taken you? You have had the complete library at your disposal, and this is all you have for me? I consider this a failure and most certainly a waste of our resources."

"Mr. Whittaker, if I could," Arnold tried to jump in. Surely he would be given some leeway given he had spent the last six weeks with a broken arm.

"I've heard enough already, Mr. Ethon. May I suggest that next time you have more detailed answers for me before I have no choice but to reconsider your access to this and any other

Spirit Wardens. You both have one week." Mr. Whittaker spun on his heel and left them in the reception area just in front of Raine.

"What an ass," Otto spoke first. He was used to acting the clown and certainly used to receiving such dressing downs, but Arnold wasn't. He hoped his dad didn't hear about this.

"One week. Does he realise I have done more reading in the last two months than I have my entire life?" He placed his hands in his pockets. "I won't know what my spirit beast's true form is until it actually shows itself."

"It teaches discipline," Raine's soft voice called across to them. "It's not about how much information you can take in. It's about the discipline of following orders and persisting at your task."

"Waste of bloody time, if you ask me," Otto shot back.

"Keep going," Raine urged. "You're both doing really well. Regardless of what Mr. Whittaker says."

"Come on, Otto, let's call it a night." Arnold set off towards the front door as he couldn't be bothered going back into the Athenaeum, feeling that this could wait until tomorrow. He had learned enough for one day.

"Boys," Raine called to them from behind her desk.

The two of them turned around to see what Raine wanted. Arnold was beginning to feel hungry and wasn't so much as in the mood for idle chat, especially after the unfair scolding he'd just received.

"Don't take it personally," Raine said. "He is like that with everyone. Some might say he has a stick up his, well, you know." She smiled at the two of them. "He has been getting a lot of grief from the Spirit Wardens about the man with the lions."

Otto sniggered loud enough for it to echo through the reception area. Arnold quickly hushed him before Mr. Whittaker heard them.

"Before you go, your dad is still in his office, Arnold. He would like you both to go up and see him before you leave." The phone rang and Raine answered, waving them away.

Arnold and Otto made their way up to Bernard's office and knocked on the door.

"Come in."

They opened the door and entered the dimly lit room. Bernard looked as though he was just finishing up for the day as he shut his laptop.

"Ah, there you are. Come with me, boys, there is something I want to show you." He moved from behind his desk and indicated for them to follow. "Right this way." The joy on his face was clear to see. He seemed excited to show them whatever it was.

They continued down the finely decorated corridor, the golden triangular pattern etched into the red carpets quickly passing them by, such was the pace that Bernard led with. They reached the reception area and Bernard placed his finger on a pressure pad in front of a door Arnold had never entered. It clicked, indicating that it had been unlocked.

"Not much further now." Bernard grinned as he held the door open and let the two of them pass him. "Keep going down this corridor to the bottom. It's the last door on the right that we're after."

Arnold could feel himself becoming giddy with the apprehension. He followed his dad's instructions and continued to the bottom of the corridor, passing a series of posh-looking vases that sat in different alcoves as they made their way to their target destination. Once he had reached the door, he stood and waited for Otto and his dad to catch up, not realising how far ahead he had got. Once they had, he placed his finger on another pressure pad, which bleeped as the door unlocked with another click.

Unable to take the apprehension any longer, Arnold

pushed the door open and walked straight through, wanting to see first what his dad wanted to show them.

The large room was empty except for the mats that lined the floor and walls as if creating a padded cell. Arnold couldn't help but feel underwhelmed at what had been revealed to them.

"This is where the next part of your training will begin," Bernard spoke to the two of them.

Arnold wondered what the next stage would entail and was just about to speak when Otto jumped in first.

"I'm not being funny, Mr. Ethon, but if you are teaching us to dance, I am out."

"As of right now, you will be coming to this very room to begin your combat training. I want you to be able to at least defend yourself should the man with the lions show his face again." Bernard walked over to the side of the door and pressed his finger against another panel. There was a loud bleep, and over by the wall, a panel slid to the side to reveal a doorway, the sleek motion representing the high standard of technology that the Spirit Wardens were in possession of.

"I have been waiting for your cast to come off, Arnold, before starting this part of your training. Please go and have a look."

"But the doctor said I had to rest," Arnold protested, although he had definitely felt the benefits of the remedy that George's granny had given him. Normally he'd be ecstatic about this next step, but after his conversation with his grandad, Arnold had felt a fearful doubt start to creep in that he couldn't explain.

"I understand that, but we cannot wait any longer. You need to be able to defend yourself. Both of you do."

Arnold and Otto made their way to the opening to have a look at what was behind the panel.

Arnold was rendered speechless. In front of them lay row

upon row of every type of close combat weaponry imaginable. Swords glistened under the lights, their steel polished so finely that Arnold could see his own reflection in them. There was a row of large spears, each individually carved from the darkest wood that Arnold had ever seen, and to the side of the room, a rack displayed various shields, each a different shape and size with animal hieroglyphs carved into them. As inspiring as the vast collection of weaponry was, Arnold also felt incredibly daunted at the sight of such things.

"We have to learn to use these?" Arnold asked, a concerned demeanour coming over him.

"Eventually," his dad replied. "You will need to train with wooden and blunted weapons first before you train with these. This is for your own safety."

"Do you think he will come back again?" Otto asked. "Do you even know where he is?"

Bernard walked over to the weapons room and picked up a spear, which he began waving around. He moved with fluidity and elegance as if he was dancing with it, demonstrating how well accustomed he was to the weapon. "We don't," he responded simply. "He has disappeared as easily as he appeared. We have no idea where he is, and that concerns me."

Bernard began to spin the spear around his body and above his head before coming to an abrupt stop and standing straight with the spear stood beside him. "I need to make sure you are prepared physically if he was to come back again. You were lucky last time, Arnold."

"You don't need to tell me, Dad. If it wasn't for your spirit beast . . ." Arnold reflected on the experience, and felt that he and his dad were closer than ever before after the attack at the hospital.

"It would be easier if we had our spirit beasts to protect us." Otto was becoming just as eager as Arnold in wanting to know what his spirit beast was.

"Well unfortunately you have not mastered your auro yet. You will have sessions around this too, but in the meantime, sticks will have to do." There was a bluntness to Bernard's comments. From time to time, Arnold knew that his dad needed to be firm with the two of them. This was one of those times.

"I nearly lost you at the hospital because we were not prepared. I will not let that happen again." Arnold's dad pulled two training swords from the rack and chucked them towards the boys. Arnold managed to catch his but was surprised by the weight, which jolted his arm and caused it to ache slightly. He stood there with the hilt of the wooden sword grasped tightly in his hand, not knowing what stance to take.

Bernard began walking down the length of the training room with his hands behind his back. "First things first. A Doyen does not kill. We capture our opponents in battle and apprehend them. This is our way. You must always remember this, no matter what. You must always keep control of your anger." He stopped to face Arnold and Otto. "Now, I want you both to try and beat me."

Arnold felt awkward – he had not had a playfight with his dad for years. "You want us to fight you with these? They're kind of heavy, Dad."

Before Arnold could continue, Otto charged at Bernard, letting out a timid attempt at a battle cry as he swung his wooden sword back and took a swipe. Bernard simply stepped to the side and laughed as Otto's momentum took him straight past him and crashing against the wall behind him.

"Your turn, Arnold." Bernard smiled.

Arnold still felt awkward and moved towards his dad with apprehension. When he reached him, he lamely stuck out his wooden sword to jab at him. His dad slapped the sword out of the way and pushed him back with both hands with more force than Arnold expected. Arnold lost his footing and stumbled backwards before falling onto the floor, causing him some discomfort as he landed on his backside.

"You have to try harder than that. The less effort you put in, the more I will push you back." Bernard stood over Arnold and stretched out his hand to help him to his feet. Arnold smiled back at his dad and decided he would up his game. He knocked his dad's hand away and then swung the wooden sword straight at his legs. Bernard lifted his leg up, easily dodging Arnold's swing.

"That's more like it," Bernard said as he stepped back and smiled at him. "Now, let's try again. Try attacking me at the same time." He turned and winked at Otto who was still smarting from clattering into the wall.

Arnold and Otto looked at each other, then ran towards Bernard. Otto had raised his wooden sword behind his head, so Arnold did the same. They positioned themselves on either side of Bernard, Arnold to the front and Otto to the rear. They continued their run and swung their training weapons with more force than the first time. Bernard stepped to the side again, and the two boys winced as the wooden swords came crashing down on each other's shoulders. Luckily for Arnold, this was on his left side and not on the side where he'd just had his cast removed.

Bernard then turned and pushed with force against them both, forcing them to fall sideways in a heap on the floor.

"Might take a while, this," Otto chuckled while climbing back to his feet. "Ow." He glanced at Arnold, evidently not appreciative of the blow he had just received.

"Same," Arnold replied as he also pulled himself back to his feet.

"This is why I need to train you. You're both clumsy and would not last two seconds in combat. I know I said that the Doyen way was to capture not kill, however if he turns up again, I want you to be able to defend yourselves and run, do you understand me? You do not try and catch him; he is far stronger and will not hesitate to kill either of you!" Bernard's seriousness was evident in his tone. "Defend and run, don't actively attack. This guy is trained and will play to your weaknesses."

Arnold and Otto's loud panting stopped as they gathered their breath. They stood side by side with their swords in hand, waiting for further instruction.

"Right, let's work on that footwork first." Bernard grabbed another training sword from the weapons room and returned to stand in front of them. "Each weapon has different footwork that you'll need to learn in order to use it as effectively as possible. For now, we will focus on the sword." He adopted a stance to show them how to place their feet, one foot pointing forward, one pointing to the side slightly behind the other.

"Copy my footwork," he demanded.

As requested, Arnold and Otto shuffled their feet into position with their training swords awkwardly by their sides. Arnold felt unbalanced by the sword and experimented with holding it in different ways to try and discover the most comfortable position.

"Try holding it the way you did when you just tried to attack me with it," Bernard hinted, seeing that they were not going to figure this out for themselves.

Lifting the weapon above his head, Arnold suddenly felt better balanced and more comfortable. Otto copied Arnold's movements and looked equally relieved to now be standing in a less awkward position.

"Hold that position. Now, take a step forward with your left foot, bringing your right foot in behind. As you do this, strike downwards with your weapon then return to your initial standing position." Bernard gave an example of the move that he wanted them to copy.

Arnold imitated the steps slowly, wanting to make sure that he got the combination right.

*Left foot, right foot, strike*, he thought to himself, concentrating on the steps to make sure the pattern stuck. He looked to his side to see Otto complete the steps with ease. Arnold knew that he would, given that he was a lot more athletic than Arnold was. He fought down the envy and focused on the task at hand.

"Again," Bernard demanded, a sternness in his voice that Arnold was not familiar with.

Arnold did as he was asked.

"Again," Bernard repeated.

When they reached the far side of the training room, they turned and went back up the hall the other way. They continued this for the next hour, patrolling the room, focusing on the footwork and the aerial strike they had been shown. Bernard stood at the side of the room, shouting out commands like a drill sergeant.

Arnold felt tired, his arms heavier than led with the weight of holding the wooden sword over the top of his head for the last hour. Bernard had been relentless and not allowed them to have a break. Arnold could feel the sweat of his face and had the thick taste of iron in his mouth. He didn't know how much longer he could continue with this. Both he and Otto had so far managed to keep up with the pace, but even Otto, who was much more physically capable than Arnold, was beginning to show signs of fatigue.

The throbbing in Arnold's right arm was tremendous and he felt as though he could feel his main vein pulsating as he continued to work through the moves. Arnold's throat felt dry and had begun to itch with thirst. He wished that the session would end so that he could get a much-needed drink.

"That's enough now, boys. Put your weapons back in the rack." Bernard clapped and appeared happy at what he had just seen them both achieve. “Well done. Take a drink and have five minutes.”

Arnold dragged himself to the weapons room to place his wooden sword on the rack. His legs felt like noodles and his right arm continued to throb from the exertion. He had never done anything like this before and he felt completely drained.

“That was great!” Otto exclaimed, clearly feeling a lot more energised than Arnold was right now.

Arnold was in disbelief at how unfazed Otto appeared to be. “How can you be feeling okay after that? I’m exhausted,” he said, still catching his breath.

“I feel great, nothing like a good workout.”

Arnold envied how easily Otto had adapted, no doubt because of his spirit beast.

Why couldn’t Arnold be more like him? Why couldn’t his spirit beast help him like Otto’s did?

Arnold couldn’t help the frustration he felt towards Otto, and he was left feeling like he was made of marshmallows, like all his bones had no structure to them anymore.

He swallowed down his jealousy, his throat still burning in desperation for a cold drink. Arnold walked to his bag and picked up a bottle of juice he had in there and gulped down the flat drink as fast as he could to quench his thirst. The sweet taste of orange replaced that of the metallic iron that he had from overexerting himself from the gruelling training exercise.

“Same again tomorrow?” Otto asked Bernard with a grin.

“We’ll be training physically three times a week from now on,” Bernard announced, a steeliness about his voice. “You’ll spend your rest days in the Athenaeum, learning how to channel your auro.”

Arnold put his drink back in his bag, the metallic taste having subsided and his breathing back to a steady rhythm. He pulled his t-shirt up to wipe the cold sweat that had collated on his forehead, leaving an inconsistent wet patch on his shirt. He understood the reasoning for needing to train this hard, but it did not mean he enjoyed it one bit.

He could only hope that with time the training would get easier – and that the man with the lions would never return for him to need it.

## CHAPTER 13

Arnold didn't really enjoy the next few weeks. The whispers and funny looks at school had settled down, but they hadn't completely stopped. He hated the fact that because he and Otto had been invited into the Spirit Wardens, most people at school started being weird around them. At least Kaden and his goons had mostly left Arnold alone since their confrontation, though Kaden would still stare at Arnold as though he was still bearing a grudge from time to time.

After school, Arnold spent his evenings carrying out more research in the Athenaeum, or being savaged in combat training by his dad. Otto had taken to it like a duck to water but Arnold just was not as fit as Otto was and he was still feeling frustrated over this. What he would give to be able to complete one training session and feel the energising buzz that Otto would drone on about at the end of each session. The good news for Arnold was that they had completed three training sessions this week, which meant there were no more for a few more days. Arnold was looking forward to going to the Spirit Wardens this evening, as they would be honing a new skill:

auro channelling. Arnold was sure this would enable him to gain a better understanding around his spirit beast.

More than ever, Arnold wanted to feel better connected with his spirit beast, and he was becoming increasingly anxious, feeling as though he was not developing as quickly as he should have been. Learning how to channel his auro was the best way he was going to discover his spirit beast, or at least he thought so anyway.

After finishing school, Arnold opted to walk to the Spirit Wardens by himself, telling Otto that he would meet him there. His jealousy of his friend was beginning to seep through as Otto seemed to be taking to life at the Spirit Wardens better than him, despite it being Arnold who had always wanted to join.

Otto trained better than him, was stronger, faster and at the moment, more eager. The perfect student.

When Arnold arrived, Otto was already waiting for him in the reception area so that they could begin their training for the day. His eagerness was beginning to make Arnold feel nauseous.

"Took your time," Otto quipped, his timing perfect as ever.

"We can't all be as perfect as you," Arnold sniped back. He didn't usually respond to Otto in this manner, but he could feel himself bubbling more than usual.

His words went straight over Otto's head, who seemed oblivious to how Arnold was feeling at the moment.

"Take a seat, boys, your dad will be down in a moment," Raine informed them, pleasant as usual as she directed the boys to a row of chairs in the reception area.

They walked across and sat in the chairs, Arnold choosing to sit on the third seat so as to leave a gap between himself and Otto. Sitting there, he began to tap his foot on the floor, something he did when he was feeling stressed or anxious. He placed his hand on his knee and attempted to consciously stop himself from doing this. He had started off really looking forward to this session but suddenly found that due to how he was feeling about Otto, he was not in the mood at all.

Around five minutes passed with neither speaking a word to each other as they waited for Arnold's dad to come and find them for today's session. Arnold continued to look at the clock, wondering what was taking him so long to come down and get them. Another ten minutes passed. Before long, Arnold had already counted each individual chequered square on the floor in front of him in an attempt to appease his boredom, the ticking of the clock almost hypnotic in the background.

"Where is he?" Arnold muttered to himself. His dad was never this late to meet them when they needed to train.

"Not like your dad," Otto added, hearing Arnold speak to himself. "Should we go over to his office?"

"Raine told us to wait here," Arnold replied.

Just then, Mr. Whittaker walked around the corridor, his manner sharp and as unhospitable as you could imagine. "Your dad can't make it this evening," he told the boys. "He's a little tied up with something at the moment. Your session this evening will be with myself. I expect nothing but concentration from you both as I do not want to be wasting my time like in the past."

"This should be fun," Otto whispered.

Arnold smiled for the first time this evening. He knew that Mr. Whittaker wasn't Otto's biggest fan, which meant he might not excel with Mr. Whittaker around.

"This way, keep up." Mr. Whittaker set off in the direction of the training room, his body language closed and cold.

They followed him down the usual corridor, ending up at the training room and entering to begin their session.

"Sit there." Mr. Whittaker pointed with his eyes, his hands arrogantly placed behind his back.

Arnold and Otto sat on the floor, waiting for Mr. Whittaker to begin.

He closed the door to the room and said, "I am told that today you are to learn more about channelling your auro. This will test you mentally and physically. If you do not feel capable of keeping up, you may stop at any time. I will be explaining the principles and it is up to you to ensure you follow my instructions. Do you both understand?" Mr. Whittaker was abrupt as usual. "I have far better things to do than be wasting my time here with you two," he added.

"Yes, sir," Arnold and Otto spoke in unison.

"Your auro is what binds your spirit beast to yourself. It is what connects you to the spirit world. Channel this and you will become more in tune, thus enabling you to have a greater connection with your spirit beast." Mr. Whittaker was walking slowly up and down the training room behind them, a calm manner about him now, his tone softer than usual. "Some people have dreams like yourself, Arnold. Others can merely feel the presence of their spirit beast. This process will help you on you journey. Now, drink this, then close your eyes and listen to my voice." He handed them both a remedy that he had prepared prior to the session.

Arnold accepted the remedy and drank it quickly. It tasted bitter and left a nasty taste in the back of his throat as if he had just swallowed a load of flowers. He closed his eyes as directed, not really knowing what to do next.

"Now I need you to think about one thing personal to you that you need guidance with, then focus on that and nothing else. I need you to remain calm, keep your breathing steady, and just stay focused." Mr. Whittaker continued to walk up and down the training room to the point where Arnold could hardly hear him taking a step.

Arnold continued to draw slow, deep breaths and began to think about what he needed guidance on. More than anything, he wanted to know that he had a spirit beast, he wanted to know what form it was. He continued to focus on this while slowly inhaling and exhaling, his body feeling more relaxed as he sat there in a semi-meditative state.

Arnold was flying. It was a strange sensation to feel like he was awake and aware of his own consciousness yet dreaming for the first time in a long time.

He wasn't in the powerful body that he'd found himself occupying in his last dream, and the surroundings were not the same as usual, however it still seemed strangely familiar to Arnold. Soaring through the sky, Arnold did not feel in control, more like a passenger. He was looking through the eyes of the spirit beast but didn't feel any of the sensations that he had become accustomed to in his dreams. He could still take in the inspiring viewpoint, his breath taken away once more like every other time he was this high up. As Arnold continued to admire the view, an arching feeling of familiarity nagged at the back of his mind, similar to when he had misplaced his phone and was re-tracing his steps to find it. Unable to shake the feeling that he knew where he was, Arnold began to focus on the buildings that were ghosting past beneath him. Whereas in his other dreams he had been flying above hills, lakes, and mountains, this time he was flying over a town. He continued to look down below to see if he recognised any of the buildings, and he spotted something: a large building which he felt as though he knew but couldn't quite put his finger on it. This time he wasn't in control of which direction he was flying, and this frustrated him greatly. He wished that they could fly down lower so he could take a closer look at the building.

Suddenly his flight path changed, and Arnold felt himself lowering down closer to the building, feeling connected to something beyond himself. He swooped down to just above it to the point where he could recognise it clearly. It was the Civic

Theatre that was just down the road from where he lived. The spirit beast was flying above Oswaldtwistle.

The flight path continued over the top of the theatre, and Arnold felt as though he was being drawn towards it like a magnet pulling the two together. He soon realised that the spirit beast was heading in the direction of the Spirit Wardens. Excitement filled his head and he felt goosebumps all over his body, his hairs on his arms standing on edge. Arnold felt certain that his spirit beast was on its way to find him, and he knew he was just about to find out its identity. He was about to connect with it – the one thing he wanted more than anything.

As the spirit beast swooped above Oswaldtwistle, Arnold saw the Spirit Wardens and felt the pull towards it. Swooping down, Arnold could feel the pull in his physical body. As he approached the Spirit Wardens, the pull felt even stronger, as though he wouldn't be able to pull away at this point even if he wanted to. A thousand horses couldn't keep him apart from his spirit beast now.

Arnold fell to his side and was promptly brought back from his dream. Dazed and confused, he sat himself back up and looked around the Athenaeum, which was still a bit of a blur, as he had been in a deep, meditative state whilst dreaming of his spirit beast. A soft glow had materialised in the room, one that Arnold instantly recognised as spirit beast energy.

Arnold scrambled to his feet, overcome with the happiness he had been longing for. He couldn't believe he was finally about to meet his spirit beast.

His eyes immediately landed on the source of the light.

Otto was glowing brightly and had a joyous look on his face, a look of real pride. In front of him stood a shining feline shape. Arnold grinned too, looking wildly around the room for his own spirit beast.

But it was nowhere in sight.

Otto's smile ran from ear to ear. "It's a leopard!" he exclaimed, overjoyed at connecting his auro to his spirit beast.

Arnold's grin faltered as he found himself playing second fiddle to Otto once again.

"I DO BELIEVE THAT IS A JAGUAR," Mr. Whittaker said. "Quite the rare spirit beast, Mr. Redburn, I'm sure your dad will be very proud." There was a hint of sarcasm in Mr. Whittaker's response towards the end of his reply.

The jaguar spirit beast sat calmly in front of Otto, and they stared intently at each other, as if taking in every tiny detail. The jaguar's tail twitched around slowly, a sign of contentment. The soft glow around it made the dark dotted pattern on its body appear even more beautiful than what anyone could have expected. Otto stepped towards the jaguar and placed his hand out towards it slowly. The jaguar nodded its head and lowered its crown, allowing Otto to make contact with it.

"It feels warm." Otto grinned as he placed his hand on the head of his spirit beast.

Arnold felt the jealousy building up inside of him again. "You just couldn't help it, could you?" he said, unable to keep the anger from his tone. "I was literally about to connect with my spirit beast when you knocked me over and broke my connection! And there you are, lapping it all up with your own spirit beast instead." Arnold knew the venom in his voice was toxic, but he'd had enough of lagging behind Otto every step of the way, and could not be bothered with it any longer. "I'm done with this, I'm done with all of it, I can't do this!" Standing up, Arnold stormed across the room, passing Mr. Whittaker along the way and shooting him a look of hatred.

"Eh?" Otto stood with his jaguar at the other end of the training room, not understanding Arnold's outburst. He looked hurt by what his close friend had just said to him, but right now, Arnold didn't care.

Arnold stomped out of the room, nearly taking the frosted glass from its casing. He walked back down the corridor at pace, his head whirling from everything that had been going on recently.

"Arnold, are you okay?" Raine asked as Arnold made his way past reception.

Arnold completely blanked her, choosing to focus entirely on the front door of the Athenaeum so that he could escape the confines of what felt like a prison. Nothing positive was happening here and he desperately wanted to be away from it.

He slid open the door and stepped outside. It was dusk, and the sun was starting to set, an orange glow filling the sky that made the clouds appear purple. Taking a deep breath of fresh air, Arnold attempted to calm himself but he couldn't. He was far too angry, and he could feel a rage building up inside of him that he did not have control of. Was this the dragon inside of him? He knew he needed to calm down and get control of his emotions.

Seeking a way to let off some steam, Arnold set off at pace and down the steps of the Athenaeum, his blood pumping and his chest heaving heavily with anger as he continued down the street. He didn't know where he was going but just knew that he needed to shake off this anger that was currently consuming him. Soon, Arnold had broken out into a jog, but his anger was not subsiding. If anything, it was getting worse.

All he could think about was how Otto had continued to progress easily, while Arnold was left to stagnate, watching his best friend get faster, stronger, better at combat, and now getting to find out what his spirit beast was. No matter how hard Arnold tried, he was always well behind his friend's progression, and it was driving him mad.

"Well, well, if it isn't Ethon," a smug voice caught Arnold's attention.

Arnold looked up and found that Kaden was standing just ahead, loitering with Piers and Caleb. Kaden stepped into Arnold's path, forcing him to stop his run.

"Not now, Kaden," Arnold said with a sternness in his voice.

"I've been wanting to catch up with you for a while. Said your girlfriend wouldn't always be around to protect you, didn't I?" Kaden teased, stepping closer into Arnold's personal space.

Arnold shook his head. Could this pompous ass seriously still be holding a grudge from a scuffle two months ago? With everything that had gone on, Arnold had completely forgotten about it. He fought to gather his breath, the frayed rope of his temper holding onto its final strings.

"I am not in the mood for this," Arnold growled, his jaw tightening as he clenched his fists fist.

"Did you hear that, boys?" Kaden laughed arrogantly before clicking his neck. "Ethon isn't in the mood." He shoved Arnold in the chest with enough force to send him backwards a few steps. "Reckon you can take me, do you?"

Blood rushed to Arnold's head, and he took a few steps towards Kaden, but then stopped himself. He had been physically training for a while now. He knew he was stronger, and overall in a better position than he was the first time Kaden picked a fight with him.

"Ooh, what are you going to do?" Kaden sneered. "You want to hit me, Ethon?" He stepped forward again, and this time so did Piers and Caleb, who smiled like a couple of accompanying hyenas.

"I don't want to fight you, Kaden," Arnold spoke slowly, yet aggressively.

"That's not what your clenched fists tell me. You think you can take me?" he jeered, looking down his nose at Arnold as if he balked at the very idea that Arnold thought he was stronger than him. Without warning, Kaden threw a sucker punch at Arnold's face, stopping inches away, wanting to intimidate him.

Arnold didn't move though. He simply stood rooted to the spot, and he would have taken the punch. He didn't, however, take kindly to it.

*Show him that you are not weak.*

Kaden laughed, looking back at Piers and Caleb, but Arnold was not going to give him a second chance. He stepped forward and threw a wild punch at Kaden. He had never punched anyone before, but it connected with Kaden's cheek, knocking him back into the arms of Piers and Caleb who stopped him from falling. Arnold's hand throbbed, but it felt good to let out his frustration.

Kaden looked on in shock and shrugged Piers and Caleb off him, his cheek reddened from the strike. He raised his clenched fists in front of him, ready to fight back, "I've got this, boys. Time to teach you a lesson, Ethon. There is a reason why you're so far down the pecking order."

Arnold wasn't fazed, and as Kaden threw a punch at him, Arnold slapped this away before jabbing him in the face again. Before Kaden had a chance to react, Arnold stepped into the space it created, then jabbed him again, and again, and again. Dazed, Kaden swung another wild punch, but Arnold slapped this away again before slamming his fist into Kaden's face once more, this time with an almighty roar of frustration. Kaden fell back into Piers before toppling to the ground.

"You're unhinged, Ethon," Caleb said, looking over a dazed Kaden.

As Arnold took a step back and took in Kaden's bloodied face, a wave of shame and guilt washed over him. Yes, Kaden was a bully, yes, he deserved it, but Arnold couldn't help but feel that he had antagonised the situation. When he saw Kaden, he wanted the fight, he had goaded the fight. A sense of dread knotted in the pits of Arnold's stomach. What had he done? Was this a sign of the dragon manifesting inside him? Was this rage and anger going to consume him?

Piers and Caleb slapped Kaden's face lightly, who responded with a dazed groan.

Piers looked up at Arnold, looking stunned. "Freak! This what they teach you in the Spirit Wardens?"

Arnold looked on in horror as panic overcame him. He turned away from the three of them and started running, through the park and into the darkness. He panted as dizzying thoughts whirled around in his head like a storm was brewing. He ran and ran, barely noticing the dark blue glow that had taken form around him. He wasn't calming down. If anything, he was getting angrier.

As he continued his run, Arnold felt his leg collide with something and he lost his footing, slamming against the ground and grazing his face and hands. He let out a loud scream, the rasp hitting him in the back of the throat, a result of his ever-building frustrations. This helped a little but did not stem the stinging sensation that had engulfed his face. Getting back to his feet and looking at the path behind him, Arnold could not see anything that may have been the cause of his fall. His foot had started to throb slightly, and he realised that he must have tripped over something.

Arnold looked back at the path again where he had fallen, but there was nothing there that he could have tripped over. He tried to gather himself, his hands and knees still stinging from sliding on the ground. He could hear the faint sound of distant cars and a dog barking as well as a light ringing in his ears due to the collision with the floor.

Suddenly Arnold found himself knocked to the floor again with a strong blow.

*Kaden,* he realised. He attempted to face his attacker but as he spun around, he took a blow to the head and everything went dark.

WHEN ARNOLD CAME TO, everything around him was blurred and he instantly recognised the dull ache in his head to be a mild concussion like he had gained a few months earlier. The room was dark and there was a dampness in the air, a musty smell that, combined with his concussion, made Arnold feel nauseous. He gazed around at his surroundings, but the lighting was limited in the room with only moonlight coming in through the gaps in the boarded-out windows scattered around. A cloud of dust could be seen dancing around in the light with no set direction, implying there were no open vents or windows.

Arnold attempted to stand up but discovered that he had been bound to a chair in his seated position. Panicking, he attempted to shout out, but someone had gagged him, and all he could muster was a muffled cry as he came to the icy realisation of his current situation.

Surely this was extreme, even for Kaden.

Terrified about what might happen to him next, Arnold's pent-up emotions got the better of him and frustrated tears rolled down his face. His eyes stinging and his cheeks wet from his tears, Arnold could feel the dust in the air sticking to his face like clingfilm. He struggled as hard and as frantic as he could to try and release himself from his constraints, but it was to no avail.

What was it that they had in store for him? What were they going to do to make him pay for what he did to Kaden? Arnold's muffled cries for help fell on empty walls. No one was around to help him, no one was around to rescue him. He had never felt so alone.

Arnold's adrenaline was soaring as his panic began to engulf him, his body trembling as he looked around for any clues as to where he was. He couldn't see enough of the room.

The door to the side of him began to creep open and Arnold's heart raced as the shadow of a strongly built figure filled the doorway. Arnold's heart sank even further when he saw who it was. It wasn't Kaden, Piers, or Caleb. It was someone much, much worse.

The man stepped forward into a dust-filled ray of light, confirming Arnold's worst fear. It was the man with the lions.

Arnold started struggling frantically. He was scared before, but this had magnified his fear by a hundred. The constraints on his arms dug into his skin, but the fear consuming him meant that he didn't notice the pain.

The man who had murdered Charles Grey – and who probably wanted to do the same to Arnold – slowly walked into the centre of the room, his footsteps echoing off the empty walls. Stopping only a few feet away from Arnold, he stood with his arms behind his back, the dust in the room dancing around him. He stood staring at Arnold with an intimidating stare, with only half of his scarred face visible due to the limited light.

Arnold wanted to ask what he wanted with him but all that came out was a muffled attempt at forming words as tears streamed down his face.

The scars across the man's cheek were smooth but dominated the right side of his face, running over his eye and down past his lips with three almost symmetrical lines. It was as though his skin had been shredded.

The man's fixed stare forced Arnold to squirm in his seat. Arnold averted his eyes, hoping to avoid eye contact with his captor, not through choice but through fear. He felt so weak and vulnerable, and there was absolutely nothing he could do right now. He was at the mercy of this murderer.

The man was breathing heavily, and with a look of fury etched across every inch of his face and his body, he continued to stare at Arnold for what felt like an eternity, each second that passed feeling like much longer than it actually was. The man's breathing began to steady to a slower rhythm as he appeared to gain control of his anger. His breaths now deep and slow, he turned and walked back out of the room without speaking a word to Arnold. The door crept shut behind him, creaking eerily.

Arnold stared at the door, expecting the man to come back, but after short period of time, he hadn't. Feeling claustrophobic from being bound to the chair and having a gag in his mouth, Arnold began to sob uncontrollably, in part from relief that the man had left without hurting him, and part from his confusion over the man's silence. He had not told Arnold why he was here, why he had taken him, or what he was going to do to him.

Arnold gathered himself by taking some deep breaths. Although petrified, he knew that sitting here crying was not going to help. He needed to try and be proactive around this situation. He had given up trying to pull his arms free, establishing that they were very much fastened to the chair and not going anywhere regardless of how hard he tried. His feet were also bound to the legs of the chair, meaning that he couldn't stand up or kick out.

Arnold began to rock the chair side to side. To his surprise, it seemed to be working, so he kept on rocking his body until eventually he had enough momentum to fall over whilst still strapped to the chair.

The chair clattered into the floor and Arnold instantly regretted his decision as his head bounced off the floor because he was unable to brace himself with his arms tied down. He could hear a strange ringing noise which he soon realised was due to the impact, and for a few moments, he felt as though his hearing was muffled.

Arnold pulled against his constraints to see if they had loosened, and to his surprise, his right hand was slightly less restrained than it was before. He began to keep pulling his right hand against the bindings. They cut painfully into his skin, but he was determined to get his arm free. He was desperate to escape this place before the man came back. His life may depend on it.

The friction burn on his arm was painful but manageable, and Arnold continued to manoeuvre his arm until eventually he was able to create a gap big enough to slide his arm back and underneath the constraints, meaning he had one arm free. He then focused on untying his other arm with his free hand, which was much easier than trying to wrestle it free. Once he had done this, he moved onto freeing his legs.

Now liberated, Arnold pulled himself to his feet, steadying himself as his concussion made him feel dizzy. Once the dizziness subsided, Arnold began walking around the room looking for any sign that would indicate where he was. The windows were all sealed with what looked like rusted metal sheets and planks of wood, and the only way out was the single door where the man had come in from just moments before. Arnold couldn't see clearly in the room and began to slowly walk across towards the door on the far side. He could hear his heartbeat and he felt wet on the side of his head. He raised his hand to touch his head and when he pulled his hand away, a stream of light that was coming into the room through the windows revealed that he had cut his head and was bleeding. The wound throbbed as he made his way to the battered door at the entrance to the room. He had no idea what he was going to do once he got out of here, but he knew he needed to try.

Something felt off, though. As much as he had injured himself breaking free from the chair, this had been too easy. Surely the man would have heard the commotion.

Arnold reached for the door to find that it wasn't locked. As he pulled it open, the slow, creaking noise made Arnold's heart race faster, the darkness in the room unforgiving and more than a little creepy.

The door opened and Arnold fell backwards. The man was

standing behind the door, listening to him this entire time, teasing, letting Arnold feel as though he had a sliver of hope to escape before cruelly snatching that hope away from him.

"You're not getting out that easy," the man hissed.

Arnold had no idea what this man wanted with him, but he was sure that he was just about to find out.

## CHAPTER 14

Otto stood opened mouthed, not fully understanding the outburst that he had just been subjected to from Arnold. Feeling confused and a little hurt by what Arnold had just said to him, he shook his head in disbelief. He had just managed to summon his spirit beast for the first time, and it should have been a happy experience. Yet he was being made to feel guilty about it, leaving him feeling conflicted. All he really wanted in that moment was for his best friend to be happy for him, but apparently since it wasn't the Arnold show, his so-called best friend was not interested, which had hurt him deeply.

"What the hell was that?" he called out, seeking some form of reassurance from Mr. Whittaker even though he knew that he wouldn't get this.

As Otto predicted, Mr. Whittaker didn't say anything at first, his silence bringing an even greater sense of awkwardness in the room.

"I suggest you find him, Redburn," Mr. Whittaker finally said. "It is in everyone's interest that Ethon remains calm. This isn't good."

Otto wanted to find Arnold, but not to calm him down as

instructed, but rather so that he could have it out with him. He couldn't let Arnold's behaviour lie. Otto couldn't believe how Arnold had been becoming more and more self-absorbed and selfish, and he felt that Arnold needed to be confronted about this before he pushed everyone away.

Near the reception area, Otto stood in the corridor wondering where Arnold might have gone. Gazing down the hall, he thought that Mr. Ethon's office might be a good place to start as Arnold may have gone to see him. Otto made his way to the office, wondering what he was going to actually say to Arnold when he came face to face with him again. When he reached the office, he noticed that the door was slightly ajar. Thinking that Arnold may be in there blowing off some steam, Otto pressed his ear against the wood, listening in case Arnold was on the other side having a rant. But all Otto could hear was a muffled sound, as though someone was talking but they were being restricted. He peeked around the corner and gasped.

Mr. Ethon was sat tied to a chair with his mouth gagged. He had a bruised eye and a trail of blood on the side of his head.

Otto burst into the room. "Are you okay? Who did this?" He moved behind Mr. Ethon and quickly untied the rope that bound him.

"What's going on here?"

Otto's dark eyes shot up to see Mr. Whittaker stood in the doorway staring straight at him and Mr. Ethon. "You, you did this!" Otto roared. "You said he was tied up with work." Without thinking, Otto stepped to the side to create a clear path between himself and Mr. Whittaker, an emerald-green glow of power emerging around him. Before he had time to think, he found himself running straight towards the Elder at speed, unable to control the rage he was feeling. He used his momentum to throw himself at Mr. Whittaker, spearing him with his shoulder.

Mr. Whittaker let out a gasp of air as he was instantly

winded. He attempted to keep his footing, but Otto's speed seemed to catch him by surprise, and as he fell backwards, the two of them clattered into the wall. Mr. Whittaker hit his head as the two hit the ground. It soon became apparent that he was unconscious.

Otto stood back up and brushed himself down, turning around and running back to Mr. Ethon to continue untying him.

Mr. Ethon continued to let out persistent muffled sounds. Otto took the hint and removed the gag from around his mouth, allowing Mr. Ethon to talk freely once again.

"It's not Mr. Whittaker!" Mr. Ethon scolded, looking shocked by Otto's actions. "He had nothing to do with this!"

"Oh," Otto said, looking across at an unconscious Mr. Whittaker. "Then who did this to you?"

"Raine."

"Raine did this? But why?" Otto asked, stunned.

"She is working with the man with the lions. She has been this whole time. Feeding him information," Mr. Ethon hurriedly explained. "Where's Arnold? Is he okay?"

"He had a blowout with me and stormed off, I came here looking for him," Otto explained, starting to become concerned about his friend's safety.

"We need to find him. They want to make him angry, they want him to release his dragon."

"Erm, he was pretty angry when he left me." Otto finished untying Mr. Ethon, and after a quick call for medical aid for Mr. Whittaker, the two of them exited the Spirit Wardens as fast as they could, looking to find Arnold and make sure that he was okay. Their concern growing, they looked at the darkened area outside and could not see any sign of him. As they ran down the steps, Mr. Ethon's worry became more and more evident on his drawn face.

Mr. Ethon pulled out his phone and began to ring his wife

to see if she had heard from him, but the phone rang out, adding to his growing fears for his son's safety. "We need to head home and see if he has gone there. My car is down here, come on."

Otto followed Mr. Ethon and the two of them dove into the car as fast as they could. Bernard's wheels spun on the spot momentarily before the tyres let out a loud screeching noise as they accelerated quickly down the road.

When they pulled up outside the house, they could see that the lights were on and the curtains remained open. Arnold's grandad could be seen in the window smiling as he stood talking to Mrs. Ethon. They clambered out of the car and ran to the house, bursting through the door.

"Arnold!" Mr. Ethon shouted, his voice breaking. "Arnold, are you here?" He moved to the bottom of the stairs as he shouted up them, hoping for a response.

"What is going on? Why are you shouting?" Mrs. Ethon walked into the hallway looking perplexed. "Bernard, what happened to your eye?"

"It's Arnold, I don't know where he is, have you seen him?" Mr. Ethon replied, panic setting in his voice. "Raine, she's been working with Charles's murderer this whole time, and I think they want Arnold. We need to find him. We need to stop them, Eve. They want to steal his spirit beast."

"They have Arnold?" Arnold's grandad entered the hall to quiz Bernard further. "Where?"

"I don't know where he could be, we never found any clues as to where the man disappeared to after he murdered Charles."

Otto looked at the adults in front of him and began to worry about Arnold's well-being, but felt equally confused as to why they would take him. Continuing to watch the ensuing conversation, Otto noticed Arnold's notepad placed on the small table at the side of the hall next to some sets of keys.

It was turned to the page containing the drawing of the tower that Arnold had dreamt about.

"Could that be any help?" Otto pointed at the pad.

"No, I already told him that I did not recognise the tower," said Bernard.

"Let me have a look." Elwood walked across to the detailed drawing. He picked up the pad to take a closer look at the sketch, and gasped. "It can't be," he said. "I know where this is, Bernard. It's too much of a coincidence . . ." A distant look appeared across his face.

"Coincidence for what?" Bernard quizzed.

Otto had no idea what they were talking about.

Elwood hesitated before answering, "It's overgrown and in a restricted area. This is a place where there are increased energy levels that link directly to the spirit world. Not many people know about it. The Elders quarantined the area a long time ago."

"I thought it was closed because of damage caused by the mines?" Bernard replied, staring at the drawing.

Elwood shook his head, looking frightened.

"How do you know about it?" Otto asked.

"Because I used to be an Elder, and it was me that sealed that place up. With good reason." Arnold's grandad tore the page from the notebook and placed this in his pocket. "We need to go right now, Bernard. I am certain that this is where they have taken him."

"I'll stay here in case Arnold turns up back at home," Mrs. Ethon said. "Bring our boy home, Bernard." Her voice shook and her eyes welled with tears. She was a picture of worry.

"I will do, Eve, I won't let anything happen to him," Mr. Ethon said. Then he and Elwood left for the front door.

Otto followed the two men outside.

"What are you doing?" Arnold's grandad pressed, a stern look across his face.

"I want to help find him!" Otto replied with an equally assertive, steely look.

"No, this is too dangerous."

"It's fine, Dad," Mr. Ethon said, "he has been completing his training. The more help we have, the better."

The three of them moved towards the car at a fast pace and jumped into the vehicle as if they had been practicing like a Formula One pitstop drill.

"Stop at my house first, I need to pick something up," Elwood requested.

They set off down the road and within a couple of minutes they were outside Elwood's house. Quickly exiting the car, Arnold's grandad ran inside and returned a few minutes later with something strapped to his back and holding some items in his hands. Otto squinted but could not make out what it was due to the darkness surrounding them. Elwood walked around the back of the car and opened up the boot before placing the items inside and closing it with a thud.

"It's been a while, Dad. You sure you remember how to use that thing?"

"Using a macahuitl is like riding a bike," Elwood said. "Now, let's go get my grandson back."

Mr. Ethon sped down the road, taking each corner as narrowly or sharply as he could, pushing the vehicle to its mechanical limits as he aimed to get to their target destination as quickly as possible. The three of them remained silent during their journey, Otto because he did not know what to say, the other two because they were trying to focus on what was ahead of them. Otto looked in the rear-view mirror and could see the worry in Bernard's eyes. He had never seen him like this before, and it rattled him.

After around twenty minutes of driving which could only be comparable to something a race car driver would have been proud of, they arrived at a heavily wooded area. As soon as the car stopped, the three of them climbed out and Otto stared into the vast darkness, unable to see past the trees that were in front of them. He could hear the sound of owls talking to each other and slight rustling coming from the bushes. Bernard and Elwood walked around to the back of the car and opened up the boot.

"Quite the collection." Bernard looked impressed at the sight of the variation of weapons that his dad had amassed and horded within his home.

"Here, thought you would like this." Elwood reached in and passed Bernard a small spear.

"My old ceremonial spear, as if you still have this." Taking hold of it, Bernard twisted it around halfway down and extended it so that it increased to a much more intimidating size. "Like riding a bike," he said, smiling.

"Otto, take this." Next, Elwood pulled out an oval-shaped shield made of a darkened wood and decorated with various carvings of different animals. "I don't feel comfortable giving you a weapon, but at least you will be able to protect yourself with this." He passed the shield to Otto who felt like a child at Christmas as he accepted it.

Otto was surprised by the weight of it, as the wood was heavier than it looked. He couldn't help but notice the faint smell of burnt cedar which must have been from the process of how the shield was made. It looked really old, and Otto couldn't help but feel that it should really be in a museum somewhere rather than in his inexperienced hands. Placing his forearm through the straps on the inside of the shield offered slightly more comfort for Otto as he pulled the shield in front of him and waited for instructions on what the next move was.

"Will this work? Seems pretty old," he said.

"You will be fine with it," Elwood reassured him. "Have you a torch, Bernard?"

"We don't need one." Bernard began to wave his hands

around and within a few seconds, his bear had been summoned in front of him, its blue glow illuminating the surrounding area and making the pathway visible for them.

"This way." Elwood led the way down the path, which wove in between the rustling trees. The bear spirit beast followed closely behind, continuing to light up the surrounding area.

The bear's light had a spectral flare to it, almost flame-like as its power kissed the darkness. It was a bizarre sight to behold. Otto wasn't used to being around spirit beasts.

The farther they walked, the more Otto's heart rate increased as his nerves and adrenaline began to take hold. He arms trembled as he crept along the path behind the others, not knowing what lay ahead of them.

They continued to navigate the path, slowly making their way through the perpetual darkness. Each step moved them closer to Arnold, Otto was sure of it.

Elwood suddenly stopped, then veered off path and began to walk through some bushes before reaching some metal fencing. "Through here, we are not that far away now." He peeled back the corner to create a small opening and gestured for Otto and Bernard to crawl through. Otto removed his shield from his arm and slid this through before following it and replacing his arm through the tight leather straps on the back of it. Once everyone was through, Otto stared at the bear, wondering how such a large spirit beast would get through the small gap. He did not have to wonder for long. The bear walked up to the fence and began to phase through it as though it wasn't there at all.

"Can I help you?" a voice demanded from the darkness.

Elwood instantly lifted his hand up to the hilt of a peculiar, paddle-like weapon, the likes of which Otto had never seen before that was strapped to his back.

Otto recognised the voice immediately. It was the unmistakable, softly spoken, reassuring voice of Raine who had always seemed so nice and polite at the Spirit Wardens. How deceiving she had been. No one would have guessed in a million years that she had been helping the man with the lions all this time. Otto was consumed by renewed shock. Why would she betray them like this? Having never felt betrayal before, a strange sensation of sadness, anger, and guilt clouded his emotions.

"Why, Raine? Why would you do this?" Bernard demanded through gritted teeth.

Raine glared at him. "Do you have any idea what it is like to be a menial?"

"I had no idea, Raine."

"That's because you never asked," she snapped. "And my name isn't Raine. It's Kiria." She stepped out from the shadows and into the light of the spectral bear. She looked completely different from what Otto was used to, appearing to be wearing some type of body armour. It looked almost like a dress but still enabled her to move with ease.

"You have no idea what it's like to be laughed at and tormented throughout school, being looked at like you have leprosy by your so-called friends. Ending up alone with no one but yourself for company, all because I am unable to summon a spirit beast." She lowered her hands to her side, her look menacing, almost like a tiger ready to pounce at any moment. "He has shown me, he has trained me."

"Shown you? What do you mean?" Otto shouted back to her. "Where is Arnold?"

"He has shown me how to take someone else's spirit beast. He has even transferred some of his power into this dagger to help me do it." Raine – Kiria, Otto reminded himself – lifted her hand to reveal a small blade that had been tucked into a holster on the side of her leg, her smile even more menacing than before.

Otto was taken a back at how different Raine looked. Far from the polite, gentle woman he had become accustomed to greeting them when they entered the Spirit Wardens, the woman before them was like an ice queen. Cold, stony faced, and aggressive. It was as though a completely different person stood in front of them.

Raine shifted her focus to Bernard's grizzly bear, a greedy expression on her face.

"That's not going to happen," Bernard said, moving himself into the path of Raine's disturbing gaze.

"Try and stop me," she returned.

Bernard placed a hand out in front of his spirit beast. "I need you to sit this one out, old friend, I can't risk losing you. We don't know what she is capable of. Dad, you go on. Otto and I will deal with Raine. You need to find Arnold, bring him home."

"*Deal* with me? DEAL WITH ME?" Raine screamed. She was losing her cool edge. "You have no idea what I am capable of, what he has taught me." Her breathing escalated as her rage seemed to take over. She ran at Bernard, jumping through the air and landing a dropkick straight to his chest. The force sent him flying backwards into the muddied path behind him. Landing on the floor on her back, Raine instantly jumped back to her feet with the precision and agility of a gymnast.

While Raine was distracted, Elwood headed down the overgrown path and disappear into the darkness in pursuit of his grandson.

Before Otto had time to think, Raine was running towards him and aiming a powerful kick in his direction. Instinctively, he lifted the shield which took the brunt of the force, with him just managing to brace himself and stop from falling over.

Raine swung her fist forward quickly. This time Otto didn't react fast enough, and the punch made a crunching noise as it connected with his cheek. Otto was shocked by Raine's strength, realising that he'd underestimated her all this time.

She seemed a lot stronger than what she should have been, especially considering she was a menial.

Raine continued her volley of assaults on Otto with a flurry of punches and kicks, her speed continuing to take Otto by surprise as each ferocious strike connected with his face, chest, and leg. Raine finalised her flurry by finishing with another blow to Otto's face, sending him crashing to the ground.

Climbing back to his feet with determination, Otto took a step towards Raine but a blur flew past him before he could act. Bernard had thrown a knee at Raine but she was able to block this and knock him away. He had preempted this and extended his spear, swinging it in the opposite way that he was moving. Raine raised a hand to parry this away before stepping back and pulling out her twin daggers.

Otto looked on in panicked awe. He thought he had been progressing well with his training, but watching the fight unfold in front of him only solidified how much further he had to go.

"I want your bear!" Raine laughed manically, as though this were a game. Her mask was well and truly off.

"How is that even possible, Raine? You're not thinking clearly. He has corrupted you."

"Corrupted me? He saved me. When I was alone, he was there for me."

Daggers in hand, Raine launched herself at Bernard and the two of them continued to dance around each other in a hypnotic rhythm. Neither seemed to be holding back, blocking each other's blows whilst equally attempting to wound the other.

Otto continued to watch, waiting for the opportune moment to help Bernard in the fight.

Bernard lunged forward with his spear but Raine stepped into the side of the extended wooden shaft and rolled into him, connecting her elbow into his sternum and causing him to stagger back.

Otto jumped in and opted to use his shield in an offensive manner, hammering the end of the it into Raine's midriff and knocking her back in return. She did not appreciate this and swung an arm up in his direction, with Otto just managing to raise his shield to protect his face. Her dagger slammed into the shield and jammed in the wood, partly splitting it. Sensing an opportunity, Otto dropped to the floor and swung a leg out, taking Raine out in the process, her ribs making a cracking noise as she slammed into the floor.

Otto jumped back to his feet and stood over Raine, enraged at how she could betray them the way that she had. "How could you do this to us?" he shouted. He was losing control as his green power surrounded him. Otto had never felt this angry before. Raising his shield above his head, he looked down at Raine who grinned back at him, looking crazed. Otto began to drop his shield towards Raine's head with as much force as he could muster. Before he had chance to connect, he found himself slammed to the floor.

"No!" Bernard screamed. "That is not our way. Capture, not kill."

"But she deserves this!" Anger and frustration pulsated around Otto along with a green tinge of energy.

"Capture, Otto, no matter what. This is the path we take. Never take a life."

"You are both so weak." Raine winced as she attempted to sit up, but she had clearly broken her ribs when she had been slammed against the floor.

Turning around, Bernard slammed the hilt of his spear into her head, knocking her unconscious instantly. "We need to move fast to get to Arnold."

"What about her?" Otto asked. He could still feel the anger inside him but felt he was able to mask this.

"You keep an eye on her," Bernard said. "I'll go and find him."

Otto sat on a tree stump a couple of metres away from where Raine lay unconscious.

Bernard hesitated. "Are you okay, Otto?" he pressed.

"I'm fine," Otto returned. "I just lost my cool, I am okay now." He pressed his shield into the ground and then leaned against it, all the while fixing his gaze on Raine. "She's not going anywhere."

Bernard nodded, then disappeared into the darkness in the direction that Elwood had headed moments earlier, his spirit beast following close behind.

Otto continued to stare at Raine. The only light around them now was that reflected by the crescent moon above them. He was so annoyed at what she had done to them, at what she had been hiding from them all this time. No wonder the Doyens had been unable to track down the man. Thanks to Raine, he'd been one step ahead of them this entire time.

Raine let out a groan as she began to come around from her unconsciousness. She began to look around and soon realised that it was just her and Otto.

She attempted to shimmy herself up, this time using the tree that was directly behind her to help sit upright. "I see that anger inside you, that rage. I've never seen any signs of that in all your time at the Spirit Wardens."

"Shut up." Otto wasn't interested in what she had to say, he had lost all respect for her.

"Bit of a personality change there, you have done it, haven't you? You have connected with it and learnt to summon it, your spirit beast." Raine's eyes lit up when she realised what had changed about him.

"I said, shut up!"

"I want to see it. Your spirit beast, what is it? I am intrigued." Raine began to talk in a flirtatious manner. "You know the old man deserved it," she purred. "Levent isn't a bad person, he just wants revenge against those that wronged him. If only you knew what they did to him, to his mum."

Otto was trying his hardest to ignore her but could feel his anger rising once more. He closed his eyes momentarily and began to take some deep breaths.

"He could help you, too, make you stronger than you could possibly imagine."

"I SAID SHUT UP!" Otto screamed at her. He had lost control of his anger and without trying, his spirit beast formed in front of him, the soft, green glow around it again lighting up their immediate environment. The intricate pattern around the jaguar's spots was like something you would see on an abstract painting. The spirit beast looked at Otto and then crouched down onto the floor. Otto was focusing on Raine, so engulfed by rage at what she had done that he had not even acknowledged that his spirit beast was there. To Otto, it was just Raine and himself. All he wanted was for her to be gone. She didn't deserve the luxury of rotting in jail, especially if anything had happened to Arnold.

"Arnold hates you, you know," Raine continued. "I mean, why would he like you? You have upstaged him every step of the way. Making him feel like he is in your shadow." She smiled at Otto. "You know the saying, 'with friends like you, who needs enemies'? Well, soon he won't be around to be a friend to anyone."

Otto's jaguar spirit beast began to crawl towards her, still crouched and ready to pounce at any moment.

"Wh – what are you doing, Otto?" Raine began to panic. "Make it stop, it's going to hurt me."

Otto barely heard what Raine was saying. He was blinded by rage and not aware that his spirit beast was creeping towards her.

As the spirit beast got close, it paused for a moment, as if teasing its prey. Then the jaguar jumped towards her.

Raine swung her dagger out from behind her and the beast roared as she buried the blade deep into its side. Otto let out a scream as he felt an excruciating pain engulf his ribs.

"Stupid boy," she gloated. "Did you think that it would be that easy?" She twisted the blade to the side, causing Otto and his spirit beast to wince. "I told you he has shown me how to steal someone else's spirit beast, and now I am going to steal yours. I will finally have one." The dagger let out an unnatural glow, and Otto suddenly felt weak, as though his energy was being drained from him. His spirit beast began to dissipate, with its spectral energy being absorbed by the blade that was embedded in its side.

Otto was consumed by panic. He could see his newfound spirit beast fading away in front of him and he felt powerless to stop it. Using what energy he had remaining, he pulled up his shield from the ground and launched it at Raine with as much force as he could muster, letting out an anguished roar. He heard a crack and a snap as it connected with Raine's head, and she limply hit the floor with a sickening thud. The blade stopped glowing and his spirit beast reappeared as his fatigue disappeared instantaneously. Otto walked over to Raine and saw that her neck was bent in an unnatural position.

She was dead.

That hadn't been his intention at all, but she was stealing his spirit beast and he didn't know what to do. His breathing grew heavy as Otto began to panic in earnest. What had he done? He had taken someone's life, something that was forbidden within the Spirit Wardens.

His spirit beast lay on its side, its breathing laboured due to the knife that was still planted firmly in its flesh. It was making a low grumbling noise, indicating it was in pain. Otto knew this as he still had a dull pain in the lower part of his ribs. He knelt next to the jaguar and placed his hand on its head in an attempt to reassure it. With his other hand, he grabbed the hilt of the blade and began to pull this from the jaguar's side. The spirit beast let out a yelp of discomfort.

The blade felt strange in Otto's hands. He could feel the energy in it as it began pulsating up through his arm from the hilt. The wave of energy intensified all the way to his shoulder until eventually he could feel this strange energy throughout his body. Otto tried to let go of the blade, but he couldn't. It was almost like the energy coming from the blade had created a reflex, preventing him from opening his hand up.

The energy coursing through his body began to overpower him. Unable to stand any longer, Otto dropped to his knees and let out an almighty scream. He was hurting everywhere and he didn't know how to make it stop. His scream echoed through the thick woodlands and only stopped as Otto collapsed on the floor, his consciousness drifting away.

# CHAPTER 15

"Sit down," the scarred man snarled. His frame filled the doorway, his persona matching the darkness that filled the room.

Seeing little other option other than to do as requested, Arnold shuffled back towards the chair, picked it up, and sat down.

"What do you want –"

"Silence!" the man interrupted, infuriated at Arnold's petulance. "You will only speak when I say it is okay to do so, do you understand? There's a lot to go through, a lot to learn, a lot to do." He stepped in through the doorframe, his large frame blocking what little light there was. "Try and escape and I will kill you. Try and sucker punch me, and I will kill you. Nod if you understand."

Arnold nodded instantaneously. This man was intimidating enough, but Arnold didn't want to risk another run-in with his lions.

A disturbing silence fell upon the room. All that could be heard was the aggressive breathing of Arnold's captor and Arnold's own panicked breaths.

After a few seconds' pause, the man continued, "That day

you stopped me from killing that coward . . . What if I told you that I'm not the bad guy in all this? That it's all a matter of perception?"

"What do you –"

"Don't answer unless I tell you to, boy!" The man slammed his fist against Arnold's leg with an incredible amount of force, his cracked face contorted with rage.

Arnold's face drained from the instant dead leg which was now throbbing along with his head. He shouldn't have said anything. After all, that's what he had been told to do, just sit and listen, but he had genuinely thought the man had paused because he was waiting for an answer. Arnold wasn't going to make that mistake again.

He stared at his captor intently and simply nodded again to indicate that he understood.

"There are two paths we can take here. One where you listen to what I have to offer and maybe live to see another day. The other involves you meeting a slow, painful end. Choose wisely," his voice rasped with rage. "You're going to find out where your loyalties lie."

This seemed like a strange statement, but Arnold opted to keep quite rather than receive another blow.

"You think it's so black and white, that I'm the bad guy, but that really is not the case. You will come to see things the way that I do. At first, I didn't realise who you were but now . . . now I know. I know what you are capable of, what you hold within you."

The man continued to prowl the room whilst he spoke. "I wasn't born from this world, you see."

Arnold felt puzzled by this statement but sure enough, the man continued to explain.

"See I am a rarity, one of a kind. There is no one else like me. You see, I was born in the spirit world."

Arnold stared blankly at his captor, wanting to ask questions. Knowing what the consequences would be if he did, he remained silent.

"As I grew up, I soon found I had the ability to switch between here and the spirit world, except initially I had no control over where I would appear in this world. This presented some . . . Let's call them challenges. As I came of age, I came to the realisation that I did not have a spirit beast connected to me. I decided I needed to find a way to have one so that I could exact my vengeance on those responsible for me being bound to the spirit world without a spirit beast to guide me."

He stopped next to the rusted panel that covered one of the many windows in the room and slammed his hand against it, the force echoing through the derelict room and prompting Arnold to jump in his seat.

"I wanted to make those that were responsible pay for their role in what happened to me and my mum."

Pulling another chair across, the man sat down opposite Arnold, his breathing not as aggressive as before. "When she explained to me about the dagger and its ability to bind spirit beasts to it, I knew I had to have it. This was my opportunity to have a spirit beast and become more powerful. She wouldn't let me have it though, not until I proved myself to her."

The man pulled out the blade in question and looked at each side of it, appearing awestruck at its appearance. "It took me many years to earn this. In that time, I managed to build a bit of a following when I was in this world. People who were amazed at my connection to the spirit world, people who were menials, who had no spirit beast connected to them. I offered to help them. Some may say it's a cult, but the most important thing is, nobody knows about us. Well, up until now. I have people everywhere, Arnold."

Placing the blade back inside his overcoat, the man continued to talk. "I know how you have struggled with connecting with your spirit beast. I know the frustrations you must be feeling because I have been there. I can help you, I can be the catalyst, the final piece of the puzzle for you finally connecting with your guide."

Arnold was intrigued but confused at the same time. If this man wanted to help him, why had he kidnapped him and tied him up? He was so desperate to have his spirit beast that he was genuinely interested in what the man was saying to him, and this worried Arnold. He knew what the man had done and what he was capable of. Arnold had to do whatever it took to survive and look at what options lay before him. What if he was able to get his spirit beast along the way?

"Outside," the scarred man demanded, "they should be here any time now, and this old tower is not the ideal place to summon a spirit beast, let alone steal one." He grinned as he led Arnold through the decrepit door and onto the barren field outside.

"This is where my story started," the man explained. By now his aggressive tone had fully subsided, replaced with an alarmingly charming manner. "It can be where yours does, too. You see, there is a powerful link between this world and the spirit world right here at this tower." Walking towards Arnold with his hands behind his back, the man calmly pointed to a tree by the side. He grabbed a flailing Arnold by his arm and dragged him to the tree before tying him to it.

The rope dug into Arnold's arms and side. There was no escaping from this. The rope was tight, the force of which made it impossible for Arnold to move his arms. "What now?" he asked before he could stop himself. He winced, expecting another blow, or maybe the long, painful death that had been promised.

Instead, the man said, "We wait. And rest assured, when you do summon your spirit beast, I am going to take it. Imagine if I had the power of a dragon that was not tethered to my soul, but to this blade!"

Arnold's heart raced to a new level, the man's plan now finally revealed. He stood bound to the tree, his body aching. He just wanted to be back home, to be safe. He wanted to know what they were waiting for.

Arnold's blood ran cold as he suddenly heard a spine-chilling scream from not so far away. He could almost feel the pain that the person must have experienced for that kind of cry.

Arnold's heart raced even faster as he began to panic. Was that someone he knew?

The man took note of Arnold's reaction, and his sinister smile returned to his face. He stood, staring intently at the entrance to the room as if waiting for someone to arrive.

Muffled shouts arose from the surrounding trees. To Arnold's surprise, his grandad appeared out of the darkness.

"Grandad!" he shouted.

Elwood's attention was drawn straight away to Arnold tied to the tree. "Arnold!" he called, racing towards him.

"Ah ah ah," the scarred man said. "I'm not finished with him yet." His demeanour completely changed once more, and his controlled aggression returned to him. "I am helping him summon his spirit beast, then I am going to rip it from his soul."

"What do you want?" Elwood demanded, coming to a halt.

The man sighed. "Did I not just explain?" Pulling his overcoat to the side, the man retrieved his blade, which started to glow. He began to wave his hands around, and soon the two lions appeared in front of him, shrouded in orange energy as they fixed their eyes firmly on their prey: Elwood.

Arnold panicked. There was nothing he could do to help his grandad, who was just an old man, no match for the lions. When Arnold had his run-in with them before, he only just survived.

"Run!" he screamed, terrified at what was going to happen to his grandad, powerless to do anything. He could feel his frustration building to anger.

Elwood turned to face the man and the beasts. "The lions of the Aether," he said knowingly. "I see that you have found a way to release them from the blade."

Elwood began to motion his hands, and Arnold knew instantly what his grandad was doing. He was summoning his spirit beast.

"I have no idea how you got that blade, I thought it was lost to the spirit world," Elwood continued as a faint blue glow emitted from him and his spirit beast began to take form.

It was an elk, with large, intimidating antlers protruding from its head. It turned to look at Elwood before turning back to face the lions. Elwood retrieved something from behind his back and revealed his macahuitl. "I am here to take my grandson back, whatever it takes."

The scarred man cracked a wicked smile. "Very well." He raised a hand, and the two lions began to run at Arnold's grandad. The elk charged at one of the lions and lowered its head, clattering into it head-on. Letting out a deafening roar, the lion bounced across the ground, eventually sliding to a stop. The second lion ran past the elk directly at Arnold's grandad who stood there calmly holding his macahuitl blade in both hands. The lion roared as it leapt through the air with its paws outstretched, ready to strike the fatal blow.

"Grandad!" Arnold called out as loud as he could.

Elwood continued to stand there calmly as the lion approached through the air. Stepping to the side at the last possible second, he raised his macahuitl and brought it down against the lion's head with such force that it was detached instantaneously from the rest of its body which came crashing down to the ground and slid to a motionless stop against the stone wall. The remaining lion let out a roar for its fallen brother and swiped at the elk, making contact with its side.

The scarred man looked furious at what had just happened and how easily Arnold's grandad had defeated one of his lions. "How dare you," he growled. "Never mind, I will have a replacement soon enough." He charged towards Elwood, bringing his blade down on him and aiming for his head, but Elwood was able to parry this with his macahuitl.

The two of them began trading blows, with each able to block the other's attacks simultaneously. Behind them, the elk and the lion continued to grapple with each other, the elk using its ginormous horns to keep the lion at bay and prevent it from being able to pounce.

Arnold remained bound to the tree, struggling in vain. He was unable to move, unable to help his grandad, and he could feel his frustrations continuing to build. He needed to help before it was too late. Yet, he was impressed at how his grandad was holding his own against his attacker. He moved as if he were still in his prime and not an elderly man.

Arnold watched as the man repeatedly tried to make contact with Arnold's grandad, but Elwood was fast enough to dodge and block his attacks.

The two of them continued with another flurry of attacks before pushing away from each other and pausing for a moment, both breathing heavily from the exchange.

"Not bad, old man, but we need to move things along." The man charged at Arnold's grandad once more. The two of them connected their weapons and began to press against one another in an attempt to get the upper hand.

"How does it feel to be back here after all this time?" the man hissed through gritted teeth. "This is where you trapped her in the spirit world."

The colour drained from Elwood's face and he momentarily

lost his concentration. This seemed to be exactly what the man was waiting for.

"How do you know?" Elwood asked.

Before he had a chance to say another word, the scarred man parried his macahuitl up into the air, spun, and planted his blade into Elwood's side.

Everything seemed to happen in slow motion. Arnold tried to scream but no noise left his mouth. This couldn't be happening, he couldn't lose his grandad, not like this, he needed to get to him. Arnold began pushing frantically against his bindings, but the thick ropes kept him firmly in his place.

The stranger pulled Elwood even closer. "I know, because the woman you trapped is my mum. I know, because she told me everything when I was born in the spirit world . . . Dad." His anger taking over once more, the man pushed his blade even deeper into Elwood's side, then released him to the ground.

Dropping to his knees, Elwood looked as though he was in shock. He was muttering to himself but Arnold could not make out what it was that he was saying.

Arnold felt powerless tied to the tree as he continued to try and escape, his blood running cold. The lion was able to overpower the elk in its weakened state and it began to dissipate back towards his grandad.

The man stood over Elwood with a look of pure hatred. "I blame you for everything, I hate you. You trapped your own wife. Do you have any idea what I have been through, what it did to me in there?" There wasn't just anger in the man's voice, there was also pain.

"I – I did not know." Elwood raised his hand and placed it against the man's face, running his fingers slowly against the scars that were gouged there. "You're my son?"

The man growled, then buried his blade into Elwood's stomach. Arnold cried out, able to see it protruding from his back. The man removed the blade and kicked Elwood over, and

Arnold's grandad lay gasping for breath, unable to talk as his mouth filled with blood.

Arnold's heart sank. He could feel his heartbeat racing and all he could feel was the anger inside him, engulfing him. He was enraged.

The murderer had stabbed his grandad and Arnold had been unable to help him. "Why would you do that!" he screamed. Arnold focused on the man, and all he wanted was to take his blade from him and make him pay for what he had done. Someone needed to stop him before he hurt anyone else, and Arnold was determined that it was going to be him.

"GET AWAY FROM HIM!" Arnold screamed, letting go of all the rage and anger that he had built up inside him. Arnold began to give off a slight glow which illuminated the darkness around him. Feeling a strong energy flow through him, Arnold felt energised, and suddenly his body had stopped aching and his fatigue instantly disappeared.

A stream of bright, blue light shot out from Arnold's chest as he let out all of his anger and rage by screaming as hard and as loud as he could. The energy began to take form. Arnold looked down and saw that the power emitting from him had slightly burned his ropes. He pulled his arms against them and was able to finally break loose. Running across to his grandad, he slid behind him and tried to prop him up. Elwood was barely conscious, but Arnold was glad that he had gotten him. Tears streamed down his face as he started to shake his grandad. "Come on, Grandad, you will be okay, just keep your eyes open."

"He has had that coming for a long time. Not as appeasing as I had always dreamed," the scarred man snarled, showing no signs of remorse for what he had just done. "Him and his friends are to blame."

"You will pay for this!" Arnold shouted, his anger and his hatred there for both of them to see. Looking to his side, he saw that his grandad's macahuitl blade was just within reach. He leaned over and picked it up, knowing what he needed to do.

Arnold stood up to confront the attacker, his hand clinched tightly to the hilt of his grandad's ancient weapon. The man stood just a few metres away with his remaining lion by his side.

A flash of light came flying between the two of them and hit the lion, knocking it over. The shape moved too fast for Arnold to see what it was, but he felt instantly connected to it.

His spirit beast had finally arrived.

"I told you I would help you unlock your spirit beast, and I have. You just needed the right motivation," the man sneered, his face distorted with anger. "Now that you have unlocked it, I am going to steal it and use it for myself. Your grandma, my mum, has a dragon spirit beast, and now I will!"

Arnold looked up at the spirit beast as it began to glide down towards him. As it came closer, he could finally see the form that it had taken, the glow around its feathers making it seem almost angelic as it lowered to him.

"Except you are wrong," Arnold said. "I don't have a dragon spirit beast like my grandma had."

"What do you mean?" The man looked up in the sky and his face became contorted with rage once more.

"It's an eagle."

The spectral eagle landed next to Arnold. Its large frame was intimidating enough, but when it spread out its wings to show an impressive wingspan, it appeared even larger. Arnold put his hand to its head and the beast lowered its crown. In that instant, the soft glow around it appeared to soothe Arnold's anger and grief for his grandad, and his mind felt clearer. His spirit beast was guiding him, and he knew he needed to follow its guidance.

"This can't be." The man was infuriated. "All the signs were there, I was told you had a dragon inside you, this can't be. I need a dragon if I'm to be truly free." His face was distorted with blind rage. "You are of no use to me, then. Look what I did to my own dad! It is going to be easy to do the same to my nephew!"

Arnold called, "It doesn't have to be like this; you don't need to hurt anyone else. There is always another way." He remembered the advice his mum had given him. "You always have a choice."

"Your grandad had a choice, too. He chose to trap his wife in the spirit world because she was too powerful. Her spirit beast took control of her and she was too strong and dangerous. Your grandad and his friends found a way of trapping her in the spirit world here at this very tower somehow."

"No," Arnold replied defiantly, "the dragon killed my grandma. Consumed her."

The man began walking towards Arnold, his dagger drawn. His lion had climbed back to its feet and now it ran past its anchor, attempting to strike out first.

"The Elder, the Doyen, the Architect, and the Soul-weaver," the man said.

The eagle flew forward and began flapping its wings with tremendous force, blinding the lion with dust. The eagle then flew at the lion with its talons and sliced the lion down its side. The lion roared and swiped at the eagle, catching its wing and sending it crashing to the floor. Arnold panicked, but his spirit beast jumped back to its feet quickly and shook itself to bring all of its feathers back into alignment.

The man reached Arnold and swiped at him with his blade, but Arnold swung the macahuitl around and was able to parry his attack away. The macahuitl was quite heavy and the weight of it surprised Arnold, even if it was made from wood and stone. His attacker followed with another strike, which again Arnold was able to parry. The man followed with a punch with his free hand, and Arnold, whose hands were both on the hilt of the macahuitl, was unable to block this in time. He took the full force in his face, staggering backwards. The man was at him straight away, his intentions clear: he wanted Arnold dead.

He swung his blade at Arnold once more, which Arnold stepped back to avoid. His attacker then aimed an aerial blow towards him, so Arnold grabbed hold of the top end of the macahuitl to turn it on its side and shield himself from the blow. A kick came through the gap, which took Arnold's breath instantaneously, knocking him back once more. The man jumped towards Arnold and aimed another fierce punch to his head, this time sending him crashing to the floor.

Arnold was in pain but knew he needed to get back to his feet quickly if he was to survive. The man was too big and too powerful for him, his combat skills far exceeding his own. To put it mildly, Arnold was simply no match for this man who claimed to be his uncle.

As the man approached, Arnold could see the glow of his own spirit beast behind him, and it flew into the back of the man's legs, tripping him to the ground. It stood in front of Arnold and placed its wings around him as if hugging him, and his pain began to fade.

Arnold climbed back to his feet, ready to face the man once more.

The man smiled at Arnold. "Back on your feet for another hiding, boy? That takes courage. I admire that. Your spirit beast is more powerful than I gave it credit for. Maybe I will take it from you after all."

"You will have to go through me first!" Bernard stood with his ceremonial spear pointed at the man. "You are a coward, attacking a teen and an old man."

Arnold's spirit lifted, his dad looking every part of the Doyen warrior he had never acknowledged. At the same time, Arnold was fearful that he would be overpowered.

Bernard's bear ran past them straight at the lion. As the two of them began to grapple, Arnold's eagle flew towards them to give aid to the bear.

The man growled before lunging at Bernard with his blade. Bernard was quick to this and parried away the attack, however he was not quick enough to block the man's fist that came crashing into the side of his jaw. Arnold leapt forward with the macahuitl and swung it with as much force as he could muster, but the scarred man blocked this with his blade before kicking him away. He swung a blow at Arnold, but Bernard's hand came across to deflect this before the scarred man swung at him. This time, Arnold blocked the attack, the man's rising frustration evident on his face.

The man jumped backwards, landing a drop kick against the two of them and knocking them both to the floor, then quickly sprang back to his feet.

"How fitting that you shall all meet your end here," he told them.

Arnold was quicker than his dad at getting up, and he ran at the scarred man with a rage inside of him. He saw his dad was climbing to his feet and the scarred man was heading towards him, his blade firmly gripped in his hand. Arnold used his dad's body as a springboard and leapt through the air, swinging his macahuitl back. He wanted to kill this murderer for what he had done.

Arnold swung the blade down and crashed its hilt against the scarred man's head, sending him slamming to the floor.

At this moment, the eagle and bear smashed into the lion, knocking it back down to the ground before the grizzly stood on its hind legs and struck down with tremendous force. The lion grumbled as it lay there, unable to climb back to its feet from its injuries.

"Now, now, brother." The scarred man gasped for breath as he climbed back to his feet, undeterred by Arnold's blow. "It's time you addressed me by my name." He paused for a moment before slowly saying the name. "Levent." He grinned, but seeing that he was outnumbered and without an active spirit beast, he stepped back towards the tower.

"Brother? What are you on about?" Bernard asked.

"I'll let the boy fill in the gaps." Levent turned to the tower and stretched his arm out. The area in front of the tower started to become distorted as if they were looking through frosted glass. He held his dagger up to the remaining lion and it began to dissipate into the blade. Running at the distortion, the man jumped towards it and simply disappeared from sight. Just like that, he was gone, and the distortion vanished.

Arnold and his dad ran at once to Elwood's side, who lay on the ground, his breathing growing even more laboured. Arnold's eagle flew across and placed its wings over the top of him to soothe his pain, but it seemed to know, as Arnold knew, that there wasn't anything else they could do. It was too late.

"I'm sorry, Bernard," Elwood gasped as his son cradled him in his arms. "It was the only thing we could do. She was out of control, and they would have killed her."

"It doesn't matter, Dad, it's okay, it will be okay." Bernard rocked his dad, trying to soothe him the best he could, his eyes filled with tears.

"I'm proud of you, son. You have raised a good boy here." Elwood smiled at Arnold. "Pass me your hand." He reached out and held Arnold's hand, placing his other hand on Arnold's chest as he closed his eyes. Arnold began to feel a strange sensation as wave after wave, a gentle, pulsating feeling came over him, emanating from his grandad.

"He's transferring his auro to you," Bernard pointed out, sniffing back the tears as he continued to comfort him.

The wave got stronger and stronger, and Arnold began to feel a little dizzy and nauseous but he managed to keep it together as he knelt on the floor by his grandad's side. Elwood smiled at Arnold and closed his eyes.

"Son, if you have something you need to say, you need to now," Bernard explained.

Arnold grabbed hold of his grandad's hand and leaned as close as he could. "I love you, Grandad." It was all he could muster but it was what he needed to tell him. He rested his head into his grandad's as his slow, laboured breath gradually came to a stop, the pulsating sensation against his body fading until he had drifted away.

Arnold had a knot in his throat, and he began to sob uncontrollably. His dad wrapped his arm around him and pulled him in tightly. The two of them began to cry into each other's arms.

"It's okay, I've got you," Bernard whispered, and they sat there together as they continued to shed tears for Arnold's grandad.

His grandad – the person Arnold loved more than anyone in this world – was gone.

# CHAPTER 16

Arnold lay on his bed at home, staring at his bedroom ceiling and thinking back on his fondest memories that he had shared with his grandad. His heart was broken. His grandad had been murdered in front of him and he had been powerless to stop it.

There was a knock on his door, and his dad entered with a glass of juice in one hand and a sandwich in the other. "I've brought you something to eat and drink. I know you don't feel like it, but you need to have something." He placed them next to Arnold on his bedside drawers and stood by the side of the bed as if offering Arnold the opportunity to talk.

When Arnold said nothing in return, Bernard turned and began to walk away.

"If only I had been able to summon my spirit beast sooner, Grandad might still be here." Arnold sat up in bed and hurriedly spat out the words. He'd had the thought in his head for the last few days.

Bernard walked back over to the end of his bed and sat down. "You can't think like that. Your grandad wouldn't want you to be beating yourself up over it. Levent knew what he was doing, and he knew that by doing what he did, he could trigger that that kind of emotional response from yourself, trigger your spirit beast." He pulled something out of his pocket and passed it to Arnold.

It was a torn photo, and Arnold instantly recognised what it was.

"We found that inside the tower. No doubt that it was left there deliberately for us."

"I know this is Grandma. I've seen the other half of the photo at Grandad's house." It was strange, finally seeing her after all this time in an old black-and-white photo. There she was with her beautiful smile, dark eyes and long, dark hair. Her hand rested just below her stomach as if she was cradling it. To her side was a small child that must have been Bernard, holding her hand tightly.

"Did you know?" Arnold pressed. "Did you know what happened?"

"I knew that your grandma was corrupted by her spirit beast and that she was gone. I did not know that your grandad found a way to trap her in the spirit world." Bernard looked conflicted with emotions. He was grieving for his dad but at the same time had learned what he and his friends had done to his mum. "I know there is no way back from corruption. If he had just told me, the burden he has carried all these years . . . Are you sure of what Levent told you? Such a gateway to the spirit world is unheard of."

"Yes," Arnold replied, wondering what his dad was alluding to.

"Corruption does not happen often, but when it does, you lose that person. The spirit beast takes over and they are not in control," Bernard explained. "As I said, there is no way back from corruption."

"So, Grandma was a prisoner then?" Arnold pressed.

"It was no one's fault what happened to her. Corruption is out of anyone's control."

"How did they trap her in the spirit world?" Arnold was even more eager to know this.

"That is the million-pound question. I have no idea. No one does, because it has never been done before." Bernard took back the old photo from Arnold and gazed lovingly at the picture of his mum. "At least in this picture we have something to remember her by now."

He stood up from the bed and again began to exit the room, placing the photograph back in his pocket.

Arnold got up from his bed, having more that he wanted to ask his dad. "What about Otto, what will happen to him?" Arnold had learned of the incident involving Raine's death, but he hadn't had a chance to speak to Otto since everything happened.

"He doesn't remember what happened," Bernard said. "He was found unconscious on the floor. However, Raine is dead, and it was his shield that did it. He will not face trial, as I can evidence that she attacked us. However, he has taken a life, which means that he will no longer be able to train at the Spirit Wardens. He will be exiled."

"What?" Arnold protested, "but –"

"The decision has already been made, and there is nothing we can do about it. Please always remember, capture, not kill. If we kill those that wrong us, we are no better than them." With this, Bernard left the room and closed the door behind him.

Arnold fell back to his bed, wondering about Otto, wishing there was something he could do for him. He picked up his phone and sent him a text, but he wasn't holding out for a reply, as Otto hadn't replied to any of Arnold's messages in the last few days since the confrontation at the tower.

Arnold ate the sandwich that his dad had brought him and had a drink of his juice before he lay back down on his bed. He wished his grandad was still here. He wished his friend would reply to him so that he could say sorry for how he had acted.

But most of all, he looked forward to seeing his uncle again so that he could exact his revenge. For in this grief, Arnold did not care for the way of the Spirit Wardens, and he knew that the next time he came face to face with Levent, he was going to kill him.

~

ARNOLD WAS free and soaring high. The sensation was amazing, and it energised every part of his body. The first few days following his grandad's death, he could not sleep, but now he was having his dreams about flying again. The air pressing against him was refreshing, like jumping into a cold pool on a hot day. He could feel the sharpness of the wind against him and the chill that came with it, all the while having the warmth of the sun against his body, giving this the perfect balance. He was high up and he was in full control. Since learning that his spirit beast was an eagle, his dreams had felt even more vivid, even more real, and the connection between the two of them was strong.

The eagle inside him had given him the strength to do the right thing against Levent on the night he killed Arnold's grandad. It had calmed his temper so that he could think clearer rather than acting on impulse.

In his dream, Arnold was in control and could fly in whichever direction he wanted. Having gotten used to his eagle body, he could soar as high as he wanted, glide as fast as he wanted, and most importantly, stop when he wanted. He loved having the control of battling against each gust of wind as it tried to halt his progress. He loved learning how to divebomb and pull up at the last second, giving him a spike of adrenaline like he had never felt before.

On this occasion, he was simply gliding, letting the wind do all the work for him. Riding each gust like a surfer in the ocean, there was a knack to it, this was an art form, and he was learning to really enjoy this.

Often, Arnold flew over unknown beautiful places, but tonight, he realised that he recognised this area and that he had been here before. He looked across the fields below and saw the tower at Rivington. But unlike on the night of the incident, the tower here didn't look old or unkept. The area around the tower was not wild and overgrown. Instead, the trees and woodlands around it appeared prosperous as if an artist had drawn them, such was the perfection of the scenery.

Tilting his wing so that he could glide down to the tower and get a closer look, Arnold began to steadily lower himself, keeping a safe distance. He began to circle the tower, and as he drew closer, he used his eagle-eyed vision to peer inside the windows, which were no longer boarded up.

Arnold could make out two people in conversation inside. One was Levent, his scarred face unmistakable. The other was a young woman with dark eyes and long, dark hair. It didn't take long for Arnold to realise who she was.

She was beautiful, much the same as in the torn photograph his dad had shown him recently.

Arnold had continued to circle, watching from afar, when he realised that the two of them had stopped talking. The woman turned to face him and looked him directly in his eyes.

In this moment, the realisation struck Arnold with absolute certainty.

She was still there, still trapped.

Arnold's grandma was alive.

# ABOUT THE AUTHOR

A.P Beswick, a devoted parent and a passionate writer, embarked on the wonderful journey of storytelling when his children expressed a desire for an original bedtime story. This story.

In 2023 A.P Beswick went full time as an author, he looks forward to sharing more of his enchanting tales with his readers. He hopes you find as much enjoyment in reading his stories as he does in creating them.

www.apbeswick.com

## ARNOLD WILL RETURN IN...

Spirit Beasts Unleashed

* 9 7 8 1 9 1 6 6 7 1 1 1 9 *

BV - #0044 - 060525 - C0 - 216/138/17 [19] - CB - 9781916671119 - Gloss Lamination